"A VETERAN AND SPECTACULAR POLITICIAN – SINGAPORE'S MR. CHAN CHEE SENG

Kim Hin David HO

Edited by Professor (Dr) Ho Kim Hin, David PhD (Cambridge),

MPhil (1st Cl Hons with Distinction) (Cambridge)

and

Dr Sun JingBo, PhD (NUS); MSc (Peking University)

PARTRIDGE

ISBN: Hardcover   978-1-5437-6656-1
           Softcover   978-1-5437-6655-4
           eBook   978-1-5437-6657-8

Disclaimer: All the contents here are not personal opinions/comments of the translator. The discrepancies, if any, in the meaning between the English and Chinese versions are due to inaccurate mapping between either languages or poor language skills rather than personal opinions of the translator.

This book in English version is translated from the Chinese version, titled *Suddenly Looking Back: Stories of Mr. Chan Chee Seng's Striving* (published in June 2015, ISBN 978-981-4671-24-8).

Print information available on the last page.

To order additional copies of this book, contact
Toll Free +65 3165 7531 (Singapore)
Toll Free +60 3 3099 4412 (Malaysia)
orders.singapore@partridgepublishing.com

www.partridgepublishing.com/singapore

This book is a dedicated autobiography and
memoir of Mr Chan Chee Seng.
Dictated originally by Mr Chan Chee Seng
Recorded originally by Mr. Zeng Guiming

CONTENTS

About the Editors

Professor (Dr) Ho Kim Hin, David, PhD (University of Cambridge), MPhil (1st Cl Hons with Distinction) (University of Cambridge), honorary professor (development economics and land economy) (University of Hertfordshire) is an honorary doctorate of letters (International Biographical Centre) (Cambridge), systems engineering (US Naval Postgraduate School), MRES (UK), AM NCREIF (US), FARES (US), MAEA (US), MESS, MSIM, and a retiree (31 May 2019 aged sixty-two years) (School of Design and Environment) (National University of Singapore). Professor (Dr) Ho Kim Hin, David, spent thirty-one years across several sectors, including the military, oil refining, aerospace engineering, public housing, resettlement, land acquisition, reclamation, and international real estate investing. Six years was spent in Pidemco Land Ltd (now CapitaLand Ltd) and GIC Real Estate Pte Ltd. Seventeen years was spent in the NUS School of Design and Environment. Estate. He holds a master of philosophy (first class honours with distinction), doctor of philosophy from the University of Cambridge, and is an honorary professor at the University of Hertfordshire (UK). He has published widely in 275 articles (inclusive of 91 articles in top peer-reviewed, international journals) pertaining to real estate investment, real estate development, public urban policy, consultancies, public- cum private-funded research projects, and so also published fifteen major books. He was a member (district judge equivalent) of the Valuation Review Board under the Singapore Ministry of Finance and the Singapore Courts. He was a governor of the St Gabriel's Foundation Singapore and a commissioner of the Singapore Scouts Association.

Dr Sun JingBo is a consultant with Deloitte & Touche LLP Singapore. She holds a master's (environment economics) (Peking University, China) and a PhD (real estate finance) (National University of Singapore). Dr Sun JingBo spent the last nineteen years across several sectors, which include economics, environmental science, real estate finance, real estate investment and development, sovereign risk model development, as well as credit risk management. She spent three years at Peking University, China, focusing on environmental economics and environmental planning and management. Four years was spent on research of residential price dynamics and consumer behaviour at the National University of Singapore. She spent two years in the real estate career as part of the strategy management group of Ascendas Private Limited Singapore and two years in Development Bank of Singapore Limited in charge of sovereign and country risk management and developing risk models. 5.5 years was spent at United Overseas Bank Singapore as a member of Credit Risk Management Group, validating all types of risk models across credit risk (exposure at default models, loss given default models, and probability of default models) at the United Overseas Bank Group level. Dr. Sun JingBo joined Deloitte Singapore three years ago. She has extensive working experiences of IFRS 9 ECL model development and audit: (1) reviewed newly developed IFRS 9 ECL models for eighteen international banks/financial institutions, (2) developed the full IFRS 9 ECL models for two international entities, (3) provided high-end consultant service and drafted original essay on IFRS 9 ECL models for several international entities (for e.g. audit the audit comments, draft an original essay on a particular topic of

PD, etc.), (4) provided IFRS 9 ECL modelling training for government officers in a south-eastern country, (5) issued four proposals for bidding international banks' IFRS 9 ECL model workshop/model development/model validation.

Being friends for half of a century, Mr Chan Chee Seng and Mr Zeng Guiming are the resource persons on this book. The background is a painting by the famous master painter, Mr Cai Mingzhi.

Preface 1

by Mr Wang Bangwen

Mr Chan Chee Seng is my old friend. When I was a secretary of People's Action Party (PAP), lots of work was assisted by passionate party members and supporters. With their passionate help, the PAP developed so fast that there was a lack of hands. Hence, I invited Mr Chan Chee Seng to help. He accepted it without any hesitation.

He was young and strong at that moment. He worked very efficiently and developed an extensive social networking. He was always able to find lots of encouraging friends to help every political publicity and election programs. He was a member in the first group of alderman voted by people, in charge of district 惹兰勿刹 for twenty-five years. Due to being born as a grassroots democracy and good relationship with the people, nobody had the courage to challenge his authority in 惹兰勿刹.

In 1961, Mr Chan Chee Seng was delegated to be parliamentary secretary by Mr Lee Kuan Yew, then Singapore's prime minister, and replaced Dr Li Shaozu. Hence, we could fight together since then. He was continuously appointed as parliamentary secretary of several ministries until 1984, when he retired. After retirement, we still met during Saturday lunches to talk about life and working life.

Mr Chan was fit and energetic with a good temper. He devoted to his own created education career after retirement. His life was really on a path like his name—'Where there is a will, there is a way.'

Although he was suffering from chronic diseases in recent years, he was still persistent and never gave up. His assistant, Mr. Zeng Guiming, volunteered to write the original book in Chinese based on Mr Zeng's dictations.

Wish all old friends of Mr Chan Chee Seng to be healthy and happy during the publication of this memoir.

Preface 2

by Mr Yi RunTang

Mr. Chan Chee Seng is a perfect student by universities and society at large.

This memoir conveys unusual stories via refreshing memories. There were no surprising, legendary, dramatic stories or complicated life game. However, it is an attractive book based on the life experiences of an eighty-plus-year-old man. It displayed struggling stories from four to eighty-three years old.

Mr. Chan's whole life was developed following his mother's one saying: 'My child, although your father died, you must be strong and brave. Friends are your teachers and helpers/supporters.' When he was five years old, he started to fight for life. His wonderful experiences were delivered in this book to encourage people.

The written style of this memoir was also unusual/special. It is not chronological. It was written freely and as Mr Chan likes. Such style saved lots of statements and verifications of the corresponding eras as the background of each story. Hence, the book has more readability.

Mr Chan Chee Seng contributed to Singapore a lot as below.

Firstly, the people love him due to his ruling for more than twenty years in 惹兰勿刹.

Secondly, he served to People's Action Party, that is, contributing to Singapore's development.

Thirdly, even after retirement, he contributed to education and established the ISS (International School of Singapore) international school and the Peking BISS international school.

As an old friend, I would like to say congratulations to Mr Chan Chee Seng for another of his achievements—this memoir.

Preface 3

by Mr Huang Shu Ren

It is very hard to find a good friend in business, more difficult in political areas. However, I was so lucky to meet Mr Chan Chee Seng in 1968. I have admired him for so many years for his treatments to friends and attitudes to life.

He treated his friends by being righteous.

To society, he strived for the utmost for his whole life to nation and to people.

To the PAP Party, he remained loyal.

He loved his life and followed the adage to 'live and learn'. Although suffering his chronic diseases, he is still positive to recall from memories about his life to finish this memoir. He delivers to us encouraging and wonderful values of life.

Thanks for his cherishing friendship for so many years.

Preface 4

by Mr Yan Chongtao

The original version was written in English. Please refer to page 14–15 in the book for details.

Preface 5

by Mr Gao Yu Chen

It happens in spring.

'Happy Rain on a Spring Night.'

'Good rain knows right season and timing, / It will fall when spring comes; along with wind it steals into night. / Mute, it moistens nature.'

This is a poem by Du Fu from China's Tang Dynasty. It tells that rain comes during spring. It captures the good timing to nourish everything. People like spring, and stories happened in spring as well.

It was in 1993 spring when I was appointed as a leader of the education bureau of Peking Chaoyang District. Via a journalist, Mr Wu Hua, I knew Mr Chan Chee Seng. He came to Peking from Singapore and would like to establish a school in Peking. I discussed with Mr Chan Chee Seng for the possibility of that project.

The district Chaoyang was a centre of political VIP, specialists, scholars, and businessmen. Their children need an international school. Therefore, Mr Chan's idea was welcome for the good timing.

We made a reservation at Peking Big Restaurant. We did not know each other at that moment, and the middleman, Mr Wu Hua, was not there. I went to the restaurant on time and saw a man stepped slowly from the upstairs. He observed that one man was in the lobby and seemed to be waiting. He just came to me and said, 'Are you Mr Gao?'

When I saw this polite gentleman, I guessed that he was supposed to be Mr Chan. I replied, 'Yes, I am. Are you Mr Chan? Nice to meet you.'

We entered into a small meeting room. Although it was our meeting for the first time, this guest from Singapore spoke Chinese like an old friend.

Mr Chan Chee Seng frankly said, 'We would like to provide international education support for China's reform and opening. We have extensive experience of international education. Today we came to Peking for establishing an international school rather than for business/profit. We will invest a lump sum amount of money for this school to contribute to children and society. We are happy to do so. Any earning in future will also be reinvested into this school as well.'

At that moment, there was no international school endorsed by the city's education bureau. We should consider from an international perspective and open the window to welcome the spring wind. I observed Mr Chan's honesty and confidence. His speech made me trust him. The negotiations/communications were undergoing in a comfortable atmosphere. After several rounds, we reached an agreement.

In 1994 spring, the first international school BISS was born in Peking. Mr Chan Chee Seng realized his dream. He could frequently visit Peking, and we had more chance to communicate.

He loved reading. Whenever he came to Peking, he always went to bookshops to search good books. He loved reading Chinese famous books and classic Chinese art. He can be quoted extensively during chatting but often said, 'I learned by myself and never entered into university. Hence, I cherish education.' He showed honesty and fabulous ideas in a gentle tone.

He was good at the education career. BISS turned into a special and beautiful school after renovation. BISS trained lots and lots of graduates who entered into famous universities all over the world.

Mr Chan Chee Seng told me that the security officers recruited for the school were not well educated, and he would like to provide them good educations. He also told me that the doctor in BISS was a heart disease specialist who also provided consultation for the neighbours around for free. I know that Mr Chan Chee Seng would like to gather all possible limited good sources to contribute to society and people. His heart and spirit were clear and touching.

Time flied, it has been twenty years since we established the BISS. BISS gained extensively good comments from students' parents and the society.

Mr Chan's career of education brought a spring wind and rain, which nourished life mutely.

2 November 2014

Preface 6

by Mr Chan Chee Seng

Friends, my teachers, helper, and supporters.

This book has been finally published.

I have never ever had the idea to publish a memoir. However, one day, when I had lunch with Bro Ming together, we chatted freely. I shared with him my past interesting suffering or experiences. In fact, some stories had been repeated. However, Bro Ming felt more and more interested. He suddenly said, 'I want to publish a memoir for you, and the name of the book is *Where There Is a Will, There Is a Way.*'

I felt shocked at that moment and replied, 'I am just a nobody, a poor guy from grassroots level and without formal education, no outstanding achievements. How dare you publish an autobiography cum memoir?'

Bro Ming said, 'Those factors are the good reasons we should publish a memoir. The memoir will be a popular book by ordinary people. I will abstract your struggles from all small or big stories in the past experiences. I saw the truth from these stories which deserves to be spread. You just talk as you like. Do not worry about the logic and lines and the order, which I will take care of.'

I was persuaded but still with hesitation. Bro Ming honestly looked at me and said, 'Chairman, I know you are modest and dislikes flamboyance. But there is one saying—"take actions when the right time comes." Please consider to publish this book for social vulnerable groups and also in order to encourage young generation and to leave a cherished life experience for people including your own children. Let us just do it.'

'Take actions when the right time comes.' It was encouraging and totally persuaded me. We made an appointment to recall memories every Tuesday afternoon in my office in ISS internal school.

I must declare again and again that if I really gained any achievements in my life, those were not by myself. In fact, my whole life, I just followed my mother's advice. When my father died, I was only six years old. My whole family suffered, and my mother told me, 'My dear child, I cannot afford to send you to school. But do not worry. You must be brave and make friends extensively. Friends are your teachers and helpers/supporters.'

Since then, I made my mind to explore by myself even when I was quite young. Since my teenage years, I made lots of friends, including people of all social strata. In my heart, there was no clear boundary between black and white. I just believed that both are just for surviving, and different people selected different ways. No matter black and white, both will reach the same destination. I totally understand both.

Once I made a friend, it was equivalent to having one more bro. I would understand their life deeper. It helped me to have a very broad point of view on human features. We need to know one another and understand one another.

I met managers of HSBC and Dutch Bank. They recruited me, such a rash young boy, to work in the banks. They were my friends and mentors. As a naive boy, I knew Mr Lee Kuan Yew, Du Jincai, Laruolenana, Wu Qingrui, etc., when I worked in HSBC. At that moment, they were not big people in political areas yet. I made them like me due to my superior banking service. I made a friend with Mr Lee Kuan Yew. We were just friends on an equal basis at that time; even I paid the bill for the beef power during lunch with him.

They prepared to build People's Action Party at that moment. It was recommended by Laruolenan, and I joined People's Action Party. Due to the friendship with them, I had the chance to be a leader in the party. All of them were my friends, mentors, and leaders in the party.

At the same moment, I also expanded to make more friends from ordinary people. They all along served the party until today. We kept being good friends. I learned a lot from them working hard for their families.

After retirement, I explored and investigated in London for six months, establishing schools and devoting to education after I came back from London. Friends persuaded me to take a rest after retirement. But I read a poem to them. 'Tomorrow, tomorrow again and again, how many tomorrows? If keep waiting for tomorrow, then nothing will be completed eventually.'

I was a layman for education. However, I am a persistent person. I started the project. The process was complicated and messy, but I had lots of help from friends. Finally, I set up an ISS international school. Twenty years ago, I entered into Peking and sang 'One Night in Beijing'. BISS in Peking made me realized that I cannot depend only on myself to run two schools. I invited experts broadly and also invited my wife, Chen Aizhen. She resigned from a good-paying job and helped me. She is the CEO for both schools until today. One poem from southern Song Dynasty came to my mind—'After endless mountains and rivers that leave doubt whether there is a path out, suddenly one encounters the shade of a willow, bright flowers and a lovely village.'

Suddenly looking back, I felt that I was lucky and had so many relatives and friends who were my teachers and mentors. The most cherished in life to me is not money and power. It was friendship. I have friends from nobody to powerful politicians and rich people. I treated them the same. It was their encouragement and help that provided me confidence all along.

Suddenly looking back, I felt that I had valuable experiences in life. I am proud to face society and friends from nobodies to people in power. Without these friends, who am I? Without all of you, I might just turn from a rash young boy to a rash old man finally. I appreciated all of you so much. My memoir is based on my eighty-two-year life experience contributing to country and to the young generation.

Being old friends for several decades, I must take this chance to say thank you to one of my old friends, Mr Guiming. He put lots of time and efforts to this book. He closely followed me from the restaurant to my office, from my office to the hospital, from the hospital to my home. He never felt and said he was tired. He knows well my spirit and thoughts. I also learned and enlightened a lot about life from his positive attitude.

Suddenly looking back, mother's saying, 'You must be brave. Friends are your teachers,' echoes in my mind.

I cannot help but reply, 'I made it, Mother. Thank you!'

Section

'Where There Is a Will'

Chapter 1

Where There Is a Will, There Is a Way

His parents named him Chee Seng, which expressed a wish, an encouragement—where there is a will, there is a way.

Mr Chan's struggles in life and legend stories proved this idea again and again. It is interesting to think of the following:

1. He does not even know 1, 2, 3, 4, 5 . . . However, he worked in HSBC and the Dutch Bank later. He was appointed to be parliamentary secretary. All these workstations were dealing with big data.

2. He was never educated in primary school. However, he was creators and operators for both ISS and BISS international schools.

3. He chaired workers brigade and provided job opportunities for high-unemployment-rate society. He built roads, did sink constructions, and took care of poor families.

4. He persuaded a sick Malay woman legislator, Madam Saborah Abmat. She had been wavering to leave her hospital bed and travel to assembly by ambulance to vote for PAP. Such voting was critical for the final result.

5. He has love and families.

Chapter 2

Mother's Tear

In 1936, in the district of Singapore called Serangoon, a young lady in an old building looked pretty but wore no smile. Her tears filled both her eyes, and all sorrow was in her face. She held a boy in her arms who looked like only five to six years old.

She said, 'My child, your father died. We are too poor to afford you to be educated.'

The boy in a stocky figure was staring at his mother and nodded. He was suffering in his heart but did not know what to say at that moment.

Mother said, 'But you must be brave and make lots of friends. Friends will be your teachers and helpers/supporters.'

The simple word by Mother guided him for his whole life and made him keep moving for the whole of his life. In his life in the future, he finally has a lot of friends.

Chapter 3

Life Is Limited, But Knowledge Is Limitless

At a Friday in June of 2014, at 7:30 a.m. in a kidney dialysis of Novena Medical Centre, an old man (eighty-two years old) was treated. He had a strong and tall figure with lots of muscles. The man was Mr. Chan, who experienced struggling stories in life.

At this moment, I was sitting in front of him, looking at him with respect and admiration. This was the hero in my heart!

He said, 'Just now I mentioned that my father died when he was young. My mother told me that valuable word. Suddenly looking back, it has been eighteen years so far. However, my mother's sorrows and tears in her eyes are still so clear up to now. Until now, I still cannot forget it. My mother's words supervised my whole life.'

Suddenly looking back . . .

Question: You paid much attention to exercise in your life. You have a habit of running around the MacRitchie Reservoir every morning. Moreover, you are the chairman of the Singapore Running Association. I have seen a famous painting by a painter named Mr Cai Mingzhi, which is displayed in your office of ISS international school. The painting portrayed hundreds of runners. The runner in the front was created by inviting you as a model. That painting rocked me.

Reply: Yes. I love that painting.

Question: You have been in good fit all along. However, you need to have the treatment of kidney dialysis this year suddenly. Can you accept it?

Reply: At the beginning, I cannot accept it and was frightened.

Question: What do you fear?

Reply: I was frightened by the wording *wash kidney*. Does it mean cut the kidney, then wash it? That is just because I did not have sufficient knowledge about kidney dialysis. However, I have learned to accept it recently. Each Friday, Wednesday, and Monday, I will do the treatment of kidney dialysis. It lasts four hours per time. During the four hours, I will enjoy delicious food and also read extensively at the same moment.

Question: This is why you are different/special. You always can convert problem to opportunity. I feel that you look great and sound healthy when you talk, totally the same as in the previous competition speech on the small truck.

Reply: Old anyway. Suddenly looking back, I will be filled with a thousand regrets more or less no matter how generous I am.

Question: Yes, people inevitably grow old. Old man inevitably will have diseases. Any advice from you, a healthy runner, to a patient young man?

Reply: Firstly, health is not a matter of course. Health is a career which you need to take the whole lifetime to develop, especially from teenagers. Keep doing exercises. Secondly, you must keep a balanced diet. Do not mess up just relying on the fact that you are still young. Thirdly, you must keep positive forever. This is helpful for psychological health.

Question: If you are saying so, you get good out of misfortune from kidney dialysis, don't you?

Reply: Taking the chance of the treatment, I can have a quiet environment and sufficient time. Hence, I read a lot. Unlike previously when I cannot read continuously or read too fast before understanding, I can read quietly and freely and realize the truth right now.

'Life is limited, but knowledge is limitless' by Zhuang Zhou. It is really true.

The painting by the famous painter Mr Cai Mingzhi.

It portrays Mr Chan as a 'running' leader.

Chapter 4

Ping Ru College Foundation for Chinese

The privacy college near to Temple of Double-Forest only taught Chinese ancient papers. When Mr Chan was a young boy, he stayed in the college for several years and learned some Chinese ancient cultures. That was the solid foundation for his Chinese, although he does not know 1, 2, 3, 4, because he was not taught it in that college.

After the war, he passed the admin exam in Chinese and became a student in Yangzheng Primary School for grades 5 and 6. After graduation, he registered in Middle School of Gongjiao. There was a blind man who was in charge of ringing the bell. But the man never missed the timing to ring the bells. From him, Mr Chan understood that 'there is good effort, there is a way'.

Question: How long have you been in Middle School of Gongjiao?

Reply: Only for grade 1 in middle school.

Question: Why not continue?

Mr Chan smiled and answered, 'Someday. The teacher told me, "You have not paid your tuition fee yet," in front of all classmates. I kept quiet and couldn't say a word. Then from the next day onwards, I never went to school. A good teacher is a soul architecture, but a bad teacher is really a damage for young souls.'

That was a real damage of the heart.

When Mr Chan was young, he was active. One of his cousins worked in a company called Guang An around South Bridge Road. He always followed his cousin to the company and helped to work here and there. He worked hard and hence was welcomed by the employees there.

Mr Chan especially loved the company of Guang An at that moment. He never knew there is a connection between him and the company of Guang An growing mutely. It affected his whole life later whether you believe or not. Let us talk about it later.

Chapter 5

10354 Japanese Factory

When Mr Chan was eight to nine years old, his sister worked in one Japanese factory and brought him there as a child worker. The factory was named 10354, which mainly produced battery for military use.

He earned 100 yen/day. That was the biggest joy for him. Also, due to his personality, he worked hard, and the manager liked him very much and called him Daro. They taught him Japanese. He was so eager to learn and could speak fluent Japanese after several years of working in the factory. Also, during the same period, a local lady named Chen Meijin taught him 1, 2, 3, 4, 5 (mathematics).

The Japanese guys were polite. They always bowed to the soldiers. One day, there was a strong and tall man who did not bow to the soldiers. One short soldier brought him crashing to the ground. Mr Chan looked at his moment and was shocked but glad. He told himself to learn Japanese judo. He established a Judo association when he was only a teenagers. He passed judo black belt very fast. Before Mr Lee Kuan Yew ruled Singapore, Mr Chan always drove Mr Lee's old-style car and accompanied Mr Lee to Malacca and Kuala Lumpur.

Mr Chan found that Japanese soldiers always forced some ladies into a modern building near the Japanese factory. The soldiers took turns to come in.

The Japanese soldiers occupied the Singapore-Malaysia peninsula for only three years and eight months. Then they surrendered. 10354 Factory also closed. The manager told him, 'There are lots of robbers at market value of 50 yen/bundle. I give them to you as a gift and also other things that you want. I will order someone to send those to your home yard and will leave the truck to you as a gift as well.'

It was a generous and huge fortune falling from the sky. It might make him a rich man since then. However, his mother seriously scolded him. 'Do not touch, okay? It is from enemy. You must not touch. Everything you cannot touch if it is generated by your work.'

Looking back that today, Mother was correct absolutely. Just imagine, after the Japanese soldiers left, how many people were staring at these fortune. If I took it, the new established government definitely would put me into prison, or I might lose my head. My mother was really wise and smart.

Chapter 6

Work Bridge

Just in 2014, when I was walking on a crowded street, one truck suddenly stopped in front of me, and the driver did not care about other cars' ringing. He quickly stepped out of the truck and shook my hand, saying, 'Mr Chan, I have spent lots of time looking for you.'

I asked him, 'Who are you?'

He replied, 'You cannot remember me? This is Da Mu from the Work Bridge. I would like to say thank you for your help. Now I am a driver of the truck and earn several thousands of dollars per month.'

Oh, he is a member of 1960 Work Bridge. At that moment, the poor salary was only SGD 1.50, but there were lots of applicants due to the high unemployment rate.

That was 1960. Singapore underwent a high unemployment rate. Mr Chan was a senator, and almost every day, there were people visiting Mr Chan to find a job. Hence, Dr Wu Wingrui discussed with Mr Chan to solve the problem.

Dr Wu said, 'Let us build a new bureau, Work Bridge, chaired by you.' Dr Wu approved the investment and appointed one financial staff to take charge of the money. Mr Chan started the work.

Mr Chan said, 'The reaction was really strong when the news was published. The poor salary was only SGD 1.5. But lots of applicants due to high unemployment rate. Due to limited budgets, we carefully started and selected forty to fifty strong men, two hundred to three hundred men during peak period.'

Work Bridge mainly cleaned streets or road or water channel and removed the advertisement posts, as well as provided food and service to some poor families.

Mr Chan said, 'Chairing the Work Bridge made me happy because it (1) offered jobs for many young men, (2) everyday helped lots of families close to grassroots levels, and (3) I became friends with grassroots classes.

Due to the needs of the work, I was allocated a jeep with a driver. It really helped. I can cross each street and visit grassroots families every day.

Recalling the memories, it seems that one potential function of Work Bridge is to establish the connection with ordinary people, which contributed to the election later.

During the peak era, there were hundreds of men in Work Bridge. Except for the headquarters, there were small stations built all over the island, and they were in charged by each of the leaders.

KIM HIN DAVID HO

However, people need more rather than only SGD1.5, which cannot afford the children's education. Hence, Mr Chan reconsidered on how to improve their living quality.

Mr Chan said the saying of Chinese famous author Lu Xun, 'Road was created by many walkers.' We proposed to select different kinds of team members and recommended to government different sectors, respectively.

He further explained, 'I just told the employer. Please accept them to work in your department for free. After working for a while, if you are satisfactory with them, you can keep them. If not, you just send them back to us.'

As a result, most of them were kept as operator of machine or driver of the truck with the payment of SGD300–400/month. Those guys brought lots of delicious food after collecting the salary and invited Mr Chan for a celebration.

One of them was the guy who stopped in front of me on the street.

It is really where there is a will, there is a way.

Chapter 7

Dutch Bank and HSBC

When Mr Chan was young, he heard one opening position in Dutch Bank. He even did not prepare and just walked in, saying, 'Sir, I would like to apply for the position.'

The recruitment manager looked at him and found that he was in a strong and tall figure with poor clothes, but there was no fear in his face.

'What kind of job would you like to apply for?'

'Sir, sorry, I do know.'

'Then are you good at mathematics?'

'No.'

'Can you do accounting or read trial balance?'

'Sorry, I cannot.'

'Then what can you do?'

'Sir, I can sweep, carry staffs, make teas or coffee, etc.'

'Young man, you got the job.' The manager was laughing.

The manager just cherished Mr Chan's honesty and confidence. When Mr Chan recalled this experience, he himself cannot help laughing. He said, 'I do not know how I dared to say that. It just felt so clear in heart and answered accordingly without any burden. That is it. I became a staff in Dutch Bank, although at the lowest level.'

As usual, Mr Chan worked hard after enrolling into Dutch Bank. Also, due to his good looks and politeness, his boss and colleagues liked him very much. More than that, a Chinese comprador from HSBC drew attention to him. After monitoring Mr Chan for a while, the comprador would like to invite him to work in HSBC.

'I would like to recommend you to work in HSBC.'

'Thank you, sir, but I am happy to work here. They treat me well.'

'Young man, this is a business era. You should strive to improve, and HSBC could pay you double.'

Wow, double salary! Mr Chan also would like to earn more and give his mother more. However, he went back home to seek for his mother's suggestion.

His mother said, 'Water always flows to the lower place. People should go to a better place. Your hard work attracted your potential employer, and you did not harm your current employer. However, you are an adult. Make your final decision by yourself.'

He joined HSBC later, like a strong fish swiped into a big river.

Due to encouragement, he worked better in HSBC. He volunteered to work in different departments. Both colleagues and customers liked and trusted him, including Mr Lee Kuan Yew, who ran a law office at that moment, Professor Du Jincai. Usually, they would send Mr Chan all the checks and papers. After they finished other stuff, Mr Chan already finished the settlements properly. The talent like him attracted people's attention. That was why he was invited to work in the People's Action Party later.

It is strange. Mr Chan did not know mathematics at all. However, he picked up something professional in HSBC. That is, when the trial balance is not balanced, all employees cannot leave and worked together to figure out the problem. Mr Chan always can find out the issue first.

'Mr Chan, please come over to help. Which number is wrong?'

'Yes, sir, I am coming.'

'Mr Chan, great!'

Chapter 8

I Am a Malay Teacher

'My dear students, welcome. You're attending this Malay module. I will try all my best to teach you Malay, our mother tongue.'

This was 1959 in the headquarters of the People's Action Party. The teacher was not a Malaysian or an expert. He was Mr Chan.

One day, Mr. Lee Kuan Yew met Mr Chan and asked him curiously, 'Is it true that you teach Malay in the headquarters? But I have never ever known you can speak Malay.'

'Yes, sir, let me tell you.'

Today, when Mr Chan talks about this experience, he still feels very proud. He said, 'How did I know Malay? I just joined PAP when I was in HSBC. Because at that moment, the government decided to select English, WU, Chinese, and Indian as four official languages of Singapore. However, there was lack of teachers of Malay. Hence, one idea came to my mind.'

'What kind of good idea?'

He said, 'There was a worker from Malaysia, Gane. I asked him to buy me two sets of Malay books for entry level. He has one set. Another set is for myself. Each time I treated him lunch, he taught me three lessons.

I will go to headquarter to teach two lessons at night. The process was repeated and repeated via learning while I taught. Who knew, more and more people came to my class finally. There were thirty to forty persons each class, including Mr Zhang Yongxiang.'

Mr Chan fought for the election later in English, Chinese, Fujian, Hainanese, and fluent Malay as well. The grassroots like him always can win.

What is the character? It is just brave but patient. That is the driver for his success in many areas later, including the critical fighting between PAP and Shenzhen in 1961. Mr Chan persuaded a sick Malay woman legislator, Madam Saborah Abmat. She had been wavering to leave her hospital bed and travel to assembly by ambulance to vote for PAP. Such voting was critical for the final result.

Mr Chan said that it is relaxing when we talk today. However, that was really stunting at that moment.

Chapter 9

Mother, Please Do Not Be Angry; Young People Love Each Other Like That

Mr Chan has two daughters. The elder one gave birth to two granddaughters and one grandson.

He married with Chen Zhenai in 1962. How did he make her fall in love with him?

Their love was rejected by the mother of his wife initially. It was tough to deal with, like a folk song from Indonesia, 'Mother, please do not be angry. Young people love each other like that.'

Question: Why was your love rejected by her mother?

Reply: The reason is that I am a poor man, but she was the elder daughter of the Company of Guang An.

Question: Is the Company of Guang An great?

Reply: Yes. It is at that moment. It is famous and well known by each family. They run the business both retail and wholesale. My wife is really a lady from a rich family. She did not live a poor life ever for one day.

Question: How did you meet her?

Reply: My elder brother worked in that company and always brought me there for fun. I lived at level 4, and the lady lived at level 2. Hence, we meet each other frequently. Hence, I won her heart because I am close to her.

Question: What is the reason for her mother's rejection?

Reply: Her father asked me, 'How can you feed my daughter? The salary for senator was only 250 dollars.' Her mother said, 'You and my daughter shared the same family name. It implied close to blood. You even did not graduate from primary school, but my daughter was well educated. How can you have the capability to take good care of her?'

Question: How did you answer them?

Reply: I am not an articulate person. I was stacked. Just said that I love her from the bottom of my heart, and I will try all my best to make her happy.

Question: I still would like to know why you had the courage to love one well-educated lady and from a rich family.

Reply: Just due to personality. It's hard to alter a man's nature.

Question: Why?

Reply: I am very persistent. Once I decided to do, I will keep doing until succeed.

Regarding this matter, I checked with Ms Chan as well.

Question: Ms Chan, why did you fall into love with him?

Reply: I was educated in Raffles Lady School. Most of the graduates will be further educated in Raffles University. However, the boyfriend of the headmistress recommended me to Victoria School, which is located in Mr Chan's district. It is just decided by fate. I cannot escape. In fact, he is from Guangdong Nanhai. I am from Guangdong Xinhui. We are not relatives.

Question: You have not answered me why you fell into love with him.

Reply: One day, several of my classmates came to the Company of Guang An for fun. When they met Mr Chan, they quickly said, 'We understand right now. You were cheated by this handsome guy.; Mr Chan was very tall and strong and handsome when he was young. Anyway, it is a fate destination or chemical reflection. We have been married for several decades. We quarrelled sometimes, but that is also another kind of interesting thing.

Do not ask me what love is.
Mother,
Please do not be angry. Young people
always love each other like that.

Chapter 10

Grassroots, Grassroots, and Grassroots

The motto of all real estate people is location, location, and location.

I describe Mr Chan as grassroots, grassroots, and grassroots. Just because of that, he succeeded whether in his career or as a man.

Mr Chan couple and I went for Maxwell foot count for lunch. All seats were occupied. Mr Chan went to the fish soup shop and spoke Teochew dialect with the boss. After a while, he went to a Hainan chicken rice shop and spoken Hainanese to the boss.

Another day, we went to ABC foot count. There were several food sellers who said hello to him. One spoke Guangdong dialect to him, saying, 'Today, we have a nice toasted baby pig. Would you like one-half? By the way, I have prepared the one weighing at around twenty grams for your preying use.'

One day, Mr Chan invited me to join a Saturday lunch party. He said, 'Come, come, all our old friends. We treat one another lunch by turn.'

The party was in a Teochew restaurant. More than ten persons were sitting on a round table. He introduced, 'This is Mr Lin. This is Ms He.' Oh god, the VIP senators in the previous Shenzhen were also old friends?

Suddenly, people said, 'Coming, he is coming.' Everyone looked at the entry. I saw him. He waved to us and said hello. He was previously cultural affairs department's Minister Yi Ren Tang.

Someone said, 'Wow, Jek still calls you Minister Yi.' He said that it was Minister Yi who appointed me to associate chairman of the Trust Bureau of National Theater. I served for nine years. I appreciated Minister Yi for his recommendation.

In 2004, Mr Chan celebrated for his BISS 10th-year anniversary. He arranged me in the nearby hotel for free. During breakfast, I entered into the restaurant with Chen Zhiyin and noticed that a whole table of guests spoke Singapore English. I took a close look beyond Mr Chan's old friends at the Saturday's lunch. There were people in the education area, the leaders of districts, entrepreneur, etc. totalling more than thirty people that Mr Chan invited from Singapore to Peking for that celebration.

There was one year, the second day after Chinese lunar new year, I was late for the appointment at the reservoir. Looking at the point, I found that more than two hundred people there. In front of them, Mr Chan held two bottles of water, shouting. I quickly joined them. Someone sent one bottle water to me. 'One two three, *satu dua tiga* new water, *merdeka!*' I stared at him. Mr Chan already was giving a speech just like the earlier competition speech. He was still charming like before.

That night, TV reported the contents. 'It is a special celebration of Chinese lunar new year. Mr Chan led several hundreds of people to celebrate in the reservoir for the new water to solve Singapore's water crisis.'

Chapter 11

Thrilling

A Vote to Save a Country

The People's Action Party was broken in 1961. Part of the members separated from the People's Action Party and established a socialism group. Not only most of the senators in the legal departments, their party branches also turned into socialism in one night, including the chairs and desk assets.

Mr Lee Kuan Yew's daughter, the head of NUS National Neuroscience Institute, wrote a paper titled 'Toast to Our Anonymous Heroes' published in *Times Streets*. There was one paragraph for Mr Chan.

The original paper was written in English. Please refer to page 57–58 for details.

I believe most of the young generation do not know the story. Even the generation who built the country might not know clearly and in detail.

Date: July 1961

Location: Legislative Assembly

Today's meeting room looks not different from other days. However, something is preparing underlying, and a big rain is coming. Twenty-five socialism senators are on one side. The other twenty-five People's Action Party members are on another side.

Today will vote for not trusting the People's Action Party. Mr Chan was on-site at that moment.

He said, 'Mr Lee Kuan Yew, Chairman Du Jincai, Secretary of Organization Department Wang Bangwen, etc., lead us to discuss.' They were all talking with a smile, calm and confident. However, everyone knew whether the People's Action Party could come into power just depended on the voting after a while.

Question: There were a total of fifty-one members. Why on the site there were fifty? Where is the other one?

Reply: In the SGH.

At that moment, all the members of the People's Action Party were anxious. Mr Chan volunteered, 'Let me find her [Sahorah]. I have a personal friendship with her.'

However, the secretary said impatiently, 'Do not do such a useless thing. Our counterparty already talked to her for several rounds.'

However, Dr Du said, 'Harry, given the personal friendship between Mr Chan and Sahorah, just let him to try.' The secretary kept silent. I just took the chance and quickly went to SGH.

Location: one ward in SGH

People: Mr. Chan and Sahorah

Sahorah: Mr Chan, I should come with you because I know you helped me a lot all along. However, I signed a letter and promised to subscribe to socialism.

Mr Chan: Do not be bound by that letter. That letter is not accepted by law. Let me tell you, socialists are free thinkers. They do not believe in any religions. Do not you worry about your religions then?

Sahorah: But if I walked out of the ward with you, they will definitely mistreat me.

Mr Chan: Do not worry. I will protect you by myself. I guarantee your safety. Trust me.

Mr Chan was not an articulate politician. But his word was very persuasive, filled in grassroots and human being characters. Sahorah's husband could not work due to poor health. Hence, Mr Chan financially supported Sahorah occasionally. Sahorah's English was poor. Mr Chan helped her to settle English documents and spent lots of time to do Sahorah's work of the selected area and people.

In addition, Mr Chan could speak Malay fluently. Hence, he can communicate with Sahorah freely. Sahorah appreciated his help and treated him as a relative. Accumulated for so many years, Sahorah trusted Mr Chan very much.

Hence, after assessing advantages and disadvantages, Mr Chan accompanied Sahorah in an ambulance to the parliament house.

Location: parliament house

All the senators sat down. All were waiting for the bell ringing. The door would be closed. One game affected the fate of the People's Action Party will be on. Both sides were holding their breaths and waiting.

Suddenly, Sahorah stepped into the room. Mr Chan followed. The bell was ringing as usual. The big door was closed.

The purdah of great career of building a country started.

Majulah Singapura, go ahead. Singapore!

Chapter 12

Any Comments until Today

Regarding the 'One Vote to Save the country', people would like to know Mr Chan's comments today on his contribution in the past.

Question: What do you feel about the event of 'One Vote to Save the Country'?

Reply: To be honest, I did not feel that thrilled at that moment. I was calm and just loyal to our party.

Question: Did you ever worry about the vote results?

Reply: I did not. I believe that is the leader's work to deal with the results. Of course, today looking back, if failed, the results will be hard to be carried. If Singapore is ruled by socialism, the investment and people's living will be different. Foreign investments must not come in. Singapore economy will be depressing always. Especially, the neighbour country, Malaysia. Indonesia has most of the Muslim. They will hammer Singapore's socialism policy. Singapore, such a small country, totally cannot resist. Hence, it will be not today's Singapore at all.

Question: You did contribute a lot at that moment. Did you get any rewards?

Reply: No. In fact, I just executed what I should do. I did it and was glad but did feel I contributed a lot. However, via this experience, I admired Dr Du Jingcai a lot because if it is not for him, nobody could persuade the chief secretary. I would not insist and go to persuade Sahorah.

Question: We know that you have different friends from different social levels and various religious sects, including the members from your counterparty party. If time flies back, will you do the same thing again?

Reply: Yes, I will.

Question: Why?

Reply: Friends are friends. Politics is politics. Different parties have different ways. Cannot go together.

Question: Did the socialism party won you over and corrupted you?

Reply: Of course they did. Not only me, they did the same thing to some other senators. He Peizhu was shifted to them. Zhang Yongxiang considered but was kept by me. Many senators in the socialism party are still our guests in the Saturday's lunch gathering.

Chapter 13

Stepping into the Political Area

When Mr Chan worked in HSBC, he knew Mr Lee Kuan Yew, Rajaratnam, Dr Du Jincai etc. Mr Chan served well. He was tall and energetic and polite. He was happy to help others. Hence, he was the right person the People's Action Party was looking for.

One day, Rajaratnam completed a form for Mr Chan and asked him to sign. Then he would join as a member of PAP.

At that moment, Mr Chan was overwhelmed and thought, *I am not a university or college graduate. I am not articulate, poor in English. I have no idea about politics at all. How come I am qualified to join the party?*

Mr Chan was glad to be recognized worthy by this Mr Big and thought, *Jobs in the party is equivalent to the work of people, to make friends as many as possible. I love this job.*

Mr Chan was always detail oriented. He sought for his mother's suggestion, then signed the form, and the nominator was Rajaratnam.

Questions: After being nominated by Rajaratnam, what did you think?

Reply: I was shocked. To be honest, I am eager to learn. I lost the normal education chance. There was imbalance in my heart. What I most want was to go to school.

Questions: Overwhelmed, excited?

Reply: Do not laugh at me. I am with no ambition at all. I have never ever thought I could be rich and become a governor via politics. However, I have a concept that I must compete the tasks well once others appointed me to do.

Questions: Any specific work after joining the party?

Reply: Yes. I was in charge of activities at the headquarters near Neil Road, including all kinds of affairs, for example, decorating the meeting room, etc. I also taught Malay in the night school of the headquarters. Mr Zhang Yongxiang learned Malay during that period.

Questions: I was promoted to an associate secretary to assist Wang Bangwen. One of the major role was to make friends extensively and select suitable people to join the party and serve the country. I met Kuang Shezhi when he was making a speech in YMCA and Cao Liying, etc. They were all recommended by me and joined the party.

Chapter 14

Trained in Israel

Question: Were you trained in Israel?

Reply: Yes. A total of three people were sent to Israel to do investigations.

Question: Anything learned?

Reply: My trip was quite an eye-opener. We visited everywhere. One day, we met a middle-aged man. He was cleaning the floor conscientiously. I admired him. After lunch, we had a class in the room upstairs. The professor was an expert of atomic energy. He entered the classroom and smiled to us. I looked to my friend and thought, Why does this man look so similar to the man who cleaned the floor? The professor said hello to us and said, 'Hello, we meet again. Welcome the friends from Singapore!' He was really the man who cleaned the floor.

Another time, we took a taxi to the dormitory. The driver was strong and of retired age. We asked him, 'Did you obtain military training?'

'Yes, sir.'

'Did you fight on the battlefield?'

'No, sir.'

'Do you have payment after retirement?'

'Yes, sir.'

'Is that enough?'

'More than enough, sir.'

'What was your ranking when you retired?'

'General, sir.'

'Wow, a general.'

These two cases illustrated that there were social strata in Israel. We felt that the people loved their country so much.

Questions: Any other observations about Israel?

Reply: Israel and Singapore are quite similar, small countries abounded by Muslim countries, and the people have a crisis mind. The policy of Israel to the neighbouring countries is eye for an eye, tooth for tooth. Israel has a galaxy of talents, well-armed military forces, and strong support by the USA. Hence, their policy is not suitable for Singapore. Singapore all along kept good relationship but proper distance with the neighbouring countries. However, there was still someone who was jealous about our achievement or challenged our international position. They used naive word to laugh at us. For example, Chen Tangshan from Taiwan said Singapore was as small as a piece of booger. The ex-president of India said that Singapore is just a red dot in the map.

Chapter 15

Special Parliamentary Secretary

Mr Chan was appointed as city senator, legislation senator, and member of parliament in charge of 诺兰勿刹区. He had strong support from the people. In the past eighteen years, almost nobody challenged. Only once, the counterparty achieved very few votes and lost guaranty money.

Mr Chan also was appointed as a parliamentary secretary to support the immigration bureau.

The chairman of the bureau was a mixed Chinese. He waited for Mr Chan at the entrance of the immigration bureau and showed him around. They arrived at level 3 and said to Mr Chan, 'Sir, this is my office. Now you take over. I will move to another one.'

Mr Chan did not consider and replied, 'Thanks, but I cannot accept your goodwill. I am used to sitting in the office.'

'Sir, what do you mean?'

'Please arrange a small room near to the lobby. I love to view people coming and going.'

'May I know why you chose an office downstairs?'

'Firstly, my voter could find me easily. Secondly, I can help the people who come here quickly. Thirdly, I am sitting in the lobby. Our staff has no dare to be lazy.'

'Well, if you insist . . .'

'What is up in his sleeve?'

In fact, there was a similar case in Japan earlier. The chairman of the Panasonic had an office near the entrance guard and looked at the staff come and go for work. He said in his memoir that he learned a lot through that experience.

At that moment, lots of bribes existed in the immigration bureau. Each day, there were lots of passport application, extension of the visa, application of EP, application of PR for foreign brides. Most of the staff only could speak English but no Chinese or any dialects. It brought trouble for people. One lady applied for his son coming into Singapore but failed again and again. Finally, the case went to Mr Chan.

Mr Chan checked with the officer for the rejection reason. The officer said that the family name of the child is Tan, but in Chinese, the father's family name was Chan. Mr Chan didn't know whether to laugh or cry. He said Chan and Tan refer to the same family name in China and Singapore Chinese.

Due to that error, the applicant waited for two years. One day, the lady gave Mr Chan a small cloth bag. Who knows, there were a bunch of one-dollar or five-dollar notes. Mr Chan said, 'This is a bribe. Would you like to put me into prison?'

The chairman of the bureau occasionally passed some complicated cases to Mr Chan. The general officer did not have no courage to make a final decision. Mr Chan carried them back home for reading. He told Wang Bangwen, 'This is not the way. They always passed me the most complicated cases. Each case has several hundreds of papers, like a book from heaven.'

'Any solution?'

'To request the officer to summarize the key points into one piece of A4-size paper. Set one cell for the governor to approval or reject.'

'Just do it.'

The idea was creative at that moment. It was very efficient to solve the previous situation, which dragged for several years or even ten years for complicated long-page cases.

Mr Chan worked as an assistant to Wu Qingrui. The media reported that Wu Qingrui criticized of public servant. 'The general psychology of being public servant is more conducted, more wrong; less conducted, less wrong; not conducted, not wrong.' However, he said that this was quite wrong.

Mr Chan closely worked with Wu Qingrui. Because Wu Qingrui was a local Chinese and could not speak Cantonese, his voters were

Chinatown people who spoke Cantonese. Hence, Mr Chan helped him to deal with the voting work. Wu Qingrui also paid attention to train the young subordinates.

He invited several officers, including Mr Chan, to his home and trained them corporate finance, advanced economics, etc. once per week. Due to the heavy work during daily time and no basic knowledge, these officers went to sleep when Wu Qingrui taught.

Mr Chan said, 'One day, we walked together around Chinatown. It was very hot. Suddenly, we saw Dr Wu drink icy juice in front of the fruit shop. Several of us quickly came over. Dr Du just said, 'Take a rest and drink some juice. I have paid mine already.' All of us were shocked and paid the money for ourselves.'

We have this consideration for one another. Such economical people were suitable to be the chairman of the finance department.

Chapter 16

City Senator and Attestation of Mayor Wang Yongyuan

Thirteen among the thirty-two positions from City Council held on 21 December 1957 were won by the candidates of the People's Action Party. Another seventeen positions were won by three different parities which were not united. Hence, the People's Action Party became the ruling party.

People were glad to have People's Action Party as a ruling party. Wang Yongyuan was mayor, and Wang Bangwen was associate mayor. The latter looked like a scholar. But who knows, he shocked the nation and the people once in the national meeting. He held a sceptre and said, 'From now on, we abolished the sceptre and English governance!' People on-site were excited and shouting at that moment. Suddenly, Wang Bangwen also turned back and pointed to the big dragon chair, saying, 'Abolish this dragon chair as well.' It made the English officer during the handing over embarrassed.

Mr Chan realized that we should not make foreigners think that we are barbarians that will lead to many conflicts. Hence, he moved the dragon chair to the original position and said, 'The new mayor is qualified to sit on it, so please take a sit!'

The show of Wang Yongyuan achieved the peoples' admiration, and the media reported extensively on the second day. Suddenly, he became a hero.

Wang Yongyuan created the Labor Park, that is, the Kallang Gym zone, which was an international airport. It turned into a blank area. Wang Yongyuan led hundreds of volunteers holding the party flags and broom to clear Labor Park.

Once, I met them on the way. I felt guilty not to attend. Wang Yongyuan smiled and said, 'You must join us next time.'

We were moved by this 'Mr Big' and replied, 'Sure, sure.'

Wang Yongyuan led the volunteers to plant, clear grasses, water the plants, etc. for several months. This action moved people. Due to the free volunteers' work, the park was named Labor Park.

The grassroots action of Wang Yongyuan popularized him for a while. He also helped to push the party to the peak period. Hence, the party won forty-three positions from the total fifty-one positions in the legislation elections. Mr Chan was also one of the winner.

Question: You were only twenty-plus-year-old when you were senator. Did you worry?

Reply: Yes. I lived in the Serangoon area. There was a famous Nansheng Park. The owner of the building was lost. It was discarded for quite a while. It was occupied by a private party as a church but for all possibilities. When I was seventeen to eighteen years old, curiously, I stepped into the building and became friends with the hoodies, especially the leader. The guy has something wrong with his spine. Hence, he can only walk using both hands and feet like a monkey. But do not look down on him. He has lots of muscles. He will attack your legs during fighting. His followers admire him very much. He fell in love with a local lady and asked me to write a love poem for the lady. How was the 'story going later'. No idea.

After a few years, I told them I will be attend the voting for senator. They were glad and said, 'We will help you and vote for you for free.'

I thanked them but said, 'Please do not use black methods. Do not scare somebody. Be polite. Do not ruin the party's reputation, please.'

They all said, 'Promised.'

Finally, these friends served as guards, and nobody threw stones. They helped a lot.

Question: Your district was complicated. Any difficulty to rule the area?

Reply: Issues and difficulties appear here and there. There were machine creator groups, the FuJian group, the famous Red Zone, and famous Amigo, cars shops, protection fees collected by different local groups. However, there were several primary schools. I have good relationships with both black and white groups. Hence, I won during the voting easily and ruled the district for eighteen years.

Question: As a senator, what are you satisfactory these years?

Reply: As a senator, I am in charge of the city fairs. I will solve lots of living issues of the people. As for the black people protection fee, it is police's work. I will not take over them. I also did not stop anybody to make a living in the area. I paid much attention to the education. I always visited the primary schools and talked to the students. Once, I visited a family and saw two young brothers. I asked, 'Are you learning in the school?' 'We just graduated from the middle school but cannot find a job.' 'Do you have good exam results?' 'Yes.' I checked their results and found really good students. 'Why do you not go to university?' 'No money.' 'You should try your best to send them to university. I will personally support you until they graduate.' The whole family appreciated me. I bought two motorbikes for them to travel to universities. These two young men became famous engineers later and contributed to the national development.

Question: Heard that you sponsored Dr Zhang in Peking to study in the USA?

Reply: Yes. Dr Zhang right now is a famous heart surgeon doctor. His wife is a nurse in BISS international school.

Question: Why do you keep contributing to education?

Reply: Maybe I just want to replace the regret that I cannot go to school when I was young.

Question: Heard that you are compassionate?

Reply: Yes. Maybe due to my poor background. My mother worked to support the whole family, and I have to work even when I was very young. Once, I saw a lady crying sitting near the drain. After checking, I understood that her wallet was stolen around Commonwealth. Now she had no idea where to go. I quickly contacted the leader of the thief and requested them to return the wallet.

He said, 'My bro, we are not lucky today. Just have a small fortune. Why do you ask us to return?'

'Today's case was a little special I met. Please just return.'

Then the lady thanked me and happily went back to Commonwealth.

Chapter 17

London Investigation and Reflection for Six Months

Mr Chan retired in 1984 at fifty-two years old. Born on 5 November 1932, he was still very energetic when he was fifty-two years old. Moreover, he accumulated sufficient life experiences at that stage.

The party provided him several positions, but Mr Chan refused.

He cared about reading and education much all along. Wu Qingrui suggested him that 'to establish an international school will be your biggest wish.'

Wu Qingrui at that moment focused on the Singapore economics development and attracted the foreign investments. Lots of foreigners checked with him whether Singapore has an international school for the second generation of professional foreigners. However, the answer was no.

Mr Chan would like to do something big in the second stage of his life to contribute to his country and people.

Hence, he went to London and stayed there for half a year.

Question: Why London?

Reply: England is a polite colonialist power of Malaysia and Singapore comparatively.

Firstly, I think the English democracy application is very successful. It is almost the best one all over the world. The ending of the ruling Malaysia and Singapore also can be deemed perfect. No violence happened. They left the city and legislation institutions. That is why the People's Action Party can govern the country so smoothly.

Secondly, Englishmen also left Singapore a complete and well system for officers, political parties, governments, and legislations as well as basic construction works, educations.

Thirdly, I also read some English classical books by Shakespeare, the modern Charles Dickens, etc. I was impressed by the English culture, the people's politeness and ethics.

Hence, I went to London and experienced these practices, and I found out how Englishmen could achieve them.

Question: Are these the macro, and any specific pointers you investigated in London?

Reply: That is education. Coz I really believed that education can contribute to the country and bring happiness to the next generations.

Questions: Any other interesting thing during the trip?

Reply: At that moment, in order to save costs, I lived in a very cheap hotel without breakfast (SGD50/week). The room does not have a toilet. I have to go outside for toilet.

Each day I had cheap and delicious breakfast around the hotel and met an Englishman at around seventy years old. He wore white clothes and carried an attaché case. He read the newspaper and had his breakfast. I walked to him and said to him, 'Good morning, sir. May I sit down?' Then we became friends, Williams. I saw him alone and having the cheap breakfast. Hence, I treated him for several times. He was happy for my treat and never treated me back. We talked a lot and freely. I like to call him Uncle William.

'Uncle William, are you working?'

'Of course, never retire.'

'Where do you work? Is the workload heavy?'

'If you like the job, you won't feel tired. I worked on the opposite street.'

I looked at the opposite street. That is an office building. I just felt exciting. Uncle William is good at observation. He checked with me. 'Do you want to take a look?'

'Sure, thank you, sir.'

I followed Uncle William and walked into the lifter. One pretty lady said, 'Good morning, gentlemen.'

I asked Uncle William, 'She greets you or me?'

'Certainly you because you are a good-looking young man!'

45

The lifter stopped at the highest level and opened. It was a specially used lifter. It was written 'William & Son Co. Ltd'. He walked ahead, and many Good morning, sirs came.

I followed him to the door and saw 'President', a very, very outstanding office. It was his—Uncle William's—office.

Mr Chan said, 'I learned what is "a man of great wisdom behaves like a fool. A man of great skill behaves like an idiot." I learned a lot of successful management experience and truth of life which are useful later.

Mr Chan walked around everywhere in London during that six months. He has a habit of observations. He will abstract the truth from the observations. He thought that the people's behaviour and characteristics are mainly a result of school education or family education.

Mr Chan always has the chance to know great men like Uncle William. One day, he was sitting in a one-star hotel nearby. He talked to a good-looking Thai guy named Pasik.

'Pasik is developing his own business at that moment and has a good net working in Bangkok. He told me that he tried to find a sponsor for building a highway from Bangkok to the airport. I wrote a letter to a Mainland China-related institution for him.'

He smiled and said, 'China finally decided to build the highway from the airport to the centre of Bangkok. Mainland China actually announced it open since 1979. Moreover, the initial stage was stopped

46

by country-held companies. Maybe they thought it is good for China's open transformation or good for relationship between China and Thailand. Anyway, the friendship between me and Pasik was solid until the end of life.'

One more thing, the project of the highway completed, I was rewarded SGD800,000. I shared half with Pasik. This was a surprise gift.

Section

"There Is a Way"

Chapter 18

ICU

Discussion of Four Chinese Classical Novels

16 August 2014 at 9:00 a.m.

I went to Tan Tock Seng Hospital.

I quietly stepped into ward 3B-25.

One old man was lying in the bed comfortably, half sleeping and half awake. He was operated in the hip. I was worrying about him. However, I suddenly realized that he was a soldier with lots of experiences.

I do not want to wake him. So I just looked around in the room. Wow. This was Singapore. There was a computer in each ward, and a professional staff was operating it. Lot of testing machines were in the ward. Many nurses and doctors were in the lobby. Maybe it was just the morning checking time.

It was my first time to step into the ICU in Singapore. I saw the advanced medical service of Singapore. It made me admire our old politician who had ever built this country for us, including the person in front here.

I heard the patient in the bed murmur, 'That is it.'

'What is that?'

'Oh, you are here.'

'Yes, sir. Good morning, Chinaman.'

'Sorry for bothering you, visiting me so early.'

'I am happy to see you look so great. Wish you recovery ASAP.'

The patient here was Mr Chan.

He was still full of humour, saying, 'The whole nation was happy to celebrate the National Day. But I devoted one harmed leg.'

'Ninth of August [National Day] is our Saturday lunch party date. Everyone went to the usual place to meet. However, I stepped on one stone and fell and broke my hip on the right side.'

By me: The machine here is first-class. How is the nurse service?

By him: Doctors and nurses are all good. One doctor asked me, 'You were educated in Chinese. May I know what the advantages of Chinese are?' I said, 'Many, many advantages of Chinese, like very profound and has a long, long cultural history. It cannot be listed completely within three days.' The doctor asked, 'You are one of the politicians who built the country. May I know how did you have the interest in the way?' I replied, 'Reading the book *The Romance of the Three Kingdoms* led me to have the initial idea.'

By him: Good question! I recently read the four Chinese classical novels *The Romance of the Three Kingdoms, Water Margin Outlaws* of the Marsh, Journey to the West, and A Dream of Red Mansions. Do you know who the author of The Romance of the Three Kingdoms is?

By me: A man named Luo Guanzhong from the end of the Yuan Dynasty. He referred to Comments on the Three Kingdoms to create The Romance of the Three Kingdoms. In total there were twenty-four volumes, finally revised by a man named Mao Zonggang in the Qing Dynasty into 120 sections.

By him: Wow, you have a good memory. To summarize, The Romance of the Three Kingdoms is actually fighting between dragon and tiger. You see, the first sentence is, 'To introduce the big matters in the world, it must be split after a long-time combination, it must be united after a long-time split.' It showed the truth of politics. From becoming brothers in the peach park to visiting Mr Zhugeliang three times to winning Zhou Yu three times to occupying Mainland with wisdom is definitely united after a long-time split. Finally, like Du Fu's poem described, 'On the sixth campaign he died, not having the grand objective met—throughout the ages, heroes are in tears, sighing with regret!'

All the people's characteristics are clear and unique in The Romance of the Three Kingdoms. Guan Yunchang's and Zhu Geliang's were the most popular.

There were Mr Guan Temple in Mainland, Taiwan, Hong Kong, or south-eastern countries where Chinese live. There is a Mr Guan statue in the lobby of big hotel or restaurant, meaning to bring safety and wealth.

In summary, *The Romance of the Three Kingdoms* shows strategies and different characteristics—bravery, loyalty, friendliness, or obedience. It is also a classical book for education and learning.

The Romance of the Three Kingdoms also shows different social strata. The poor people lived suffering. Sometimes, I can feel the same as them. It also made me more close to our people. Hence, it equipped me for politics life.

Du Fu saw lots of Mr Guan temples, but not many Mr Kong Ming temple (Zhu Geliang). One day, he went to Cheng Du and found one old Mr Kong Ming temple. Hence, Du Fu wrote the following poem:

DU Fu—The Premier of Shu

中文原文：

丞相祠堂何處尋？
錦官城外柏森森，
映堦碧草自春色，
隔葉黃鸝空好音。

三顧頻煩天下計，
兩朝開濟老臣心。
出師未捷身先死，
長使英雄淚滿襟。

英文翻譯/English Translation:

Where lies the shrine commemorating the renowned premier of Shu? On the outside, the Magnificent City is surrounded with groves of cypress trees.

The terrace contrasts the spread of green lawn painting a field of spring,

Through the foliage comes orioles singing, in vain in seems.

His hut was frequented thrice over; he was sought after two warring states pacify.

He gave his heart and soul in helping his master and son establish a state of ideals.

Yet he died before his military expeditions for unity could succeed,

His regret often has those of similar aspirations weep tears of grief.

Note: Mr Kong Ming Temple in Cheng Du has been innovated beautifully by the Chinese government and serves for tourism.

The Romance of the Three Kingdoms will trigger you to appropriate and consider. No matter Europe or USA or China, Asia including Singapore is filled in political battles. When I was young, I read these books. And birds of the same feathers flock together. Many of my friends are similar as me. We worked for the party. I have no regret for my life like that.

By me: What do you feel about *Water Margin Outlaws of the Marsh*?

By him: In sum, the *Water Margin Outlaws of the Marsh* is forced to climb up Mountain Liang. Do you know who the author is?

By me: When I was in middle school, classmates gave me a nickname Cai Zi ('a man with profound knowledge'). I always can get 100 scores in examinations. Lots of legends about the author of *Water Margin Outlaws of the Marsh*, but the correct should be Shi Naian from the Yuan Dynasty, Luo Guanzhong revised. Jin Shengtan from the Ming Dynasty deduced that Luo Guanzhong wrote continuously after section 70 onwards.

By him: Really admire you. You have a good memory. Look at *108 Heroes*. All are heroes from all different ways. The most impressive story is *Lin Chong Run at Night*. There are lots of violence and anti-violence. We also read the experience of grassroots. We had the same feeling, and it made us more close to the people. All of these are sensitive to a politician.

By me: *Journey to the West* is described as a cartoon of Western journey. The author is Wu Chengen. He collected all the *Journey to the West* stories from the Tang, Song, Yuan, and Ming Dynasties and Monkeys. The common person read it as a general novel with wisdom and humour. What do you feel and interpret?

By him: *Journey to the West* is a wonderful book which deserves to be read more than one hundred times. Later, if Western moviemakers apply Western advanced science to make several movies based on *Journey to the West*, it will be much, much popular than *Harry Potter*.

I summarized one sentence for *Journey to the West* as 'a myriad of rivers and thousands of hills are all BUDA'. Mr Tang accepted the appointment and went West for *Bible Book of BUDA*. He had thousands and thousands of suffering during the journeys, but he insisted to carry on and finally got the *Bible Book of BUDA*. If summarized in Chinese, it would be, 'There is a will, there is a way.' I was educated by my mother and *Journey to the West*. No matter, my education career or politics career were affected.

Once set a target, no matter how persistent to achieve it, *Journey to the West* also sheds light on the philosophy of BUDA.

By me: To me, the book *A Dream of Red Mansions* is most difficult to read. So far, I have not finished reading the whole book yet. The first eighty sections were written by Cao Xueqin from the Qing Dynasty. The second forty sections were written by Gao E, who was thirty years younger than Cao Xueqin. What do you think?

By him: I have the same feeling as you. *A Dream of Red Mansions* is a profound book. It looks like a book about ladies/beauties. However, most poems were fabulous. In my eyes, A Dream of Red Mansion is 'a great family's decadence']. The book provided a warning to people that a family or nation, no matter rich or powerful, if lacking of good governance, will finally decay. Modern countries showed lots of *A Dream of Red Mansions* stories, aren't they?

By me: Chainman Chan, the conversation made me admire you more. It is not reading for ten years. It should be reading each day in the life. Toast for you.

Chapter 19

A Hero Does Not Easily Shed Tears until His Heart Is Broken

At 11:30 a.m. on 19 Aug 2014

I entered into ward 6D-29. Mr Chan had been moved from the ICU to this room.

I read the four classical Chinese novels to him before his families came.

He said, 'I suddenly recalled that I was almost died twice when I was young. Both times were saved by my mother. One day, I was sick and cannot eat/drink. Having high fever, I looked thin and yellow. My mother held my hand to go to Chinatown for preparing. But on the way, I cannot persist. My mother let me take a rest, saying, 'Don't worry. Mother knows God will save you, but you must be in front of him.'

I nodded. Then I went with Mother again. (Mr Chan was sad and missed his mother. He had tears in his eyes and tried to control his emotion in front of me.) Then he murmured, 'My mother . . . we went ahead, and both of us were sweating. My mother still encouraged me and said, 'Good boy, carry on, please. Remember there is a red bean soup in Chinatown which you like very much. Carry on, my boy. Mother will buy the soup for you once we arrive.'

In fact, we did not have money for medicine. That was why we walked from home to Chinatown rather than taking the bus. How could we buy a red bean soup? However, mother really bought a red bean soup for me that day. Mr Chan almost cried when he talked about this.

He continued, 'There was a temple near the residence. According to the local people, the lady has powers. After I drunk the ashy water, I was really cured. As I recalled the experiences today, I think it might be due to long walking and sweat. That helped me be cured. Or the red bean soup works?

'Another time, I had dengue fever and felt freezing all over the body. Again, I drunk the ashy water and recovered. Mr Chan said, 'My mother . . .'

Chapter 20

All Twinkle, Twinkle Little Stars in the Sky

An eighty-two-year-old man with a strong figure was lying in the bed in the hospital, looking at the sky, and clearly reading 'Twinkle, twinkle Little Star, how I wonder what you are?'

At 9:30 a.m. on 2 September 2014.

I entered into ward 6D-76. At the first glance, I saw Mr Chan lying in the bed. Behind him was his wife, Chen Aizhen. I asked her, 'Mrs Chan, why you are so early today?'

She smiled and answered, 'Today I am in charge of breakfast.'

'What did you buy for his breakfast?'

'Soy milk and sugar cake.'

'Mr Chan does not like the food of the hospital?'

'Totally refuse.'

Maybe due to my voice, Mr. Chan woke up and looked at me. 'Good morning, Chairman.'

He arranged me to sit down in front of him. His wife took this chance to say, 'Okay, since somebody came and took over, I am going to leave. Bye.'

'I will have a chat freely today.'

A nurse came in and said, 'Morning, sir. Can we do the physio now?'

'Let's do it later. I have a VIP visitor here. How about one hour later?'

Mr Chan looked at me, saying, 'They took turns to come in for this test and that test. So much bother. Even I cannot sleep well.'

'This is a Singapore hospital. They cherish every patient. Especially you are a VVIP, how dare they do not work hard.'

'Ha ha, VVIP's blood vessel is difficult to be found as a common men. Yesterday, a doctor tried several times and made me very painful. I scolded him.'

'I also had the similar experience and found that the senior nurse is more skilful than a doctor.'

Mr Chan is a just person. He always like to help others especially the grassroots class. Sometimes he was excited. But the past experiences told him to be calm. He looked strong and tall. But actually, he took care of the details. He observed, listened, and made decisions in his heart.

'Gui Ming, I told you last time how I fell into love with my wife. At that moment, she was a little girl. Her little sister was too young. I had two little dogs. One was dead in a traffic accident. The other one was missing. Until now, I am doubting that it was pushed into the river by my wife's little sister.'

I asked, 'Why?'

He said, 'I guess that it should be due to jealousy. The little sister loved to play with me. But I loved to play with the dog. Hence, she was jealous. I lost my dog and very sad. I think dogs are loyal friends to people, and sometimes they are better than human beings.'

I said, 'If that is just what you guess, please forgive the little sister coz she was very young.'

He said, 'If not, what else can I do? All my wife's younger sisters and brothers treated me well and loved to play with me. The love between my wife and I accumulated with time. Until one day, I have not seen her for several months and found that I seemed to lose something. Hence, I suddenly realized that I fell into the love with her. I felt I cannot live without her. Such feeling lasted until now. People say that it is happy to have lovers and friends when we are old. So I am very happy now.'

That was the first time I saw his direct expression of his love. The eighty-two-year-old hero experienced a complicated life, and he was showing gentle love suddenly. It was touching.

I changed the topic and asked him, 'The operation in your right leg is so successful, and you can walk so soon.'

He said, 'It is really ironic. My both legs were hurt, which was related to food. Several years ago, my wife went to Hang Zhou. My granddaughter came and invited me for a dinner. I was in a hurry and fell when I turned. My left thigh was hurt.'

I said, 'Yes. At that moment, I was with Wang Huimin, a CEO of Hang Zhou JiangNan, a colleague, for a dinner, and Ms Chan. Ms Chan was very calm after receiving the call from your daughter. She did not say anything to us until the night flight from Peking to Singapore. She told us that you hurt your leg.'

Mr Chan continued, 'Do you believe? Do you have any religion?'

He said calmly, 'Many people persuaded me to trust Jesus. But until now, I cannot believe God created everything. Due to the twice experiences surviving from the prepaying and saved from illness. I trust BUDA naturally.'

He continued, 'Maybe because I was from a grassroots level and always helped poor men even I am not rich as well. That is why BUDA protected me and both my granddaughters who graduated from BISS international school and got offers from NUS, NTU, Hong Kong University, and Sydney University. Both of them selected Hong Kong University finally. I financially sponsored both my granddaughters using my savings. Nobody requested me to do so. I did this and felt happy. Nothing is more important than happiness.'

He was energetic and still would like to talk until noon.

Staring outside through the windows, he said, 'I love to be alone, driving the car to seaside. Looking at the sea and looking up to the sky—where is the heaven, which was played messy by the monkey sun?

'Twinkle, twinkle little star, how I wonder what you are? What is the answer, you ask me? I ask my heart, "How big the heart, how big the love. How big the heart, how big the world."'

Chapter 21

The Most Happiness Is Having Granddaughters and Sons

Many years ago, one of my good friends told me, 'You know, I have a long journey in my life. Later, I have a terrace and a car. But I found that that cannot make me happy. When I had my first daughter, I communicated with her. That made me feel very happy.'

At that moment, I was very young and thought that 'such a great man and complicated life. How come turned to be so emotional.'

Until ten years ago, my daughter lived in Hong Kong and gave a birth to a baby named Jenny. I also accompanied with her grow and flew to Hong Kong to play with her. At that moment, I suddenly realized that my old friend's saying was correct. The most happiness is to have granddaughter/sons.

I asked Mr Chan, 'Do you have the same feeling?'

He smiled and said, 'My granddaughter is named Yu An, twenty years old. She studies in Hong Kong University. My second granddaughter named Yu Xin, eighteen years old, also studies in Hong Kong University. Both graduated from BISS international school. The third grandson is fifteen years old, studying in BISS right now for level 10. The ancient saying is 'Pearl on hand cannot describe my love to my three granddaughters/sons. I would like to say nothing is happier than to have granddaughters/ sons.'

He said, 'My three granddaughters/sons are all close to me. Their attitudes towards life were affected by me. They occasionally send me postcards. Their regards make me feel warm, and I will tell myself. Everything deserved.'

Mr Chan smiled and passed a dozen postcards to me. 'Look, you will know what I am feeling.'

Chapter 22

Head Bowed, Like a Willing Ox I Serve the Children

'Chairman Chan, I found that when you talk about your three granddaughters/ sons and your ISS and BISS international school and students, you brighten up with joy. Why?'

'Yes. You observed correctly. Each time I talked about these, I felt so happy. I loved next generations due to being a grassroots and being loved by my mother when I was young. I remember a poem by Lu Xun, 'A Satire on Myself'.

Original Poem in Chinese

运交华盖欲何求,
未敢翻身已碰头。
破帽遮颜过闹市,
漏船载酒泛中流。
横眉冷对千夫指,
俯首甘为孺子牛。
躲进小楼成一统,
管他冬夏与春秋。

A Satire on Myself
Lu Xun

Born under an unlucky star,

What could I do?

Afraid to turn a somersault,

Still my head received a blow.

My face hidden under a torn hat,

I cross the busy market.

Carrying wine in a leaking boat,

I sail downstream.

Eyebrows raised, coldly confronting

Accusing fingers of a thousand bullies.

Yet with my head bowed,

I'll be an ox for children.

Secluded in my small attic,

I'll enjoy my solitary state.

Who cares if it's winter or summer?

Who cares if it's autumn or spring?

（中国文学出版社　编译）

Self-Mockery
Lu Xun

There's nothing you can do about a hostile fate:

You bump your head before you even turn.

When in the street I pull my old hat down;

My leaky wine-boat drifts along the torrent.

Coolly I face a thousand pointing fingers,

Then bow to be an infant's wiling ox.

Hiding in our little house, sufficient to ourselves,

I care not what the season is outside.

(W. F. Jenner 译)

'Yet with my head bowed, I'll be an ox for children. Secluded in my small attic, I'll enjoy my solitary state.' That impressed me a lot.

ISS and BISS international schools were established thirty-five and twenty years ago, respectively. More children were coming from fifty different countries from kindergarten to grade 12. Thousands and Thousands of students came and left. I served and devoted happily.

Chapter 23

An English Dictionary under the Road Light

Along a road. A road light was gloomy.

At midnight, one twelve- to thirteen-year-old boy was standing under the road light and held a book. Occasionally, he touched his head and searched for something in a dictionary.

When he fully focused on reading the book, two twenty-five to twenty-six-year-old men came behind him. One said, 'Do not move. Raise your hands.'

Another man said, 'Mr Chan, what are you doing under the road light at midnight?'

Mr Chan looked at these two persons and gladly said, 'Do not pretend. I met lots of bad hat since I was young. You two do no sleep at home at midnight. What are you doing here?'

Both guys said, 'We missed you coz we have not seen you for the whole week. We thought you were sold by someone.'

'Why did you not even say goodbye before you left? And never came to Guang An?'

'I feel uncomfortable because I was looked down on.'

'You mean the owner looked down on you?'

'No.'

'I know, you mean another two staff?'

'Yes.'

'That bad man always fight with others. Do not care about him.'

'I know. I heard that he always said someone has the food for free.'

'I said, it is not your food. Why do you care?'

Mr Chan finally said, 'I know the guy referred to me. In fact, I worked so hard every day. Why it is having food for free? I know the guy looking down on me. Mother told me that we should keep a decent distance from the food when having dinner and only took the food near to me. Each time I had dinner with them, I am always feeling frightened and no courage to have the dishes. They always eat very fast. Only left some soup for me, but I still eat the leftover with rice. What most hurt my heart is that he looked down on me and said I eat for free in Guang An. Hence, I came home.'

'Mr Chan, we know that. But it does not matter if somebody looked down on you. If you do not look down on yourself, everything will be okay. You are only a teenager now, and you will have a bright future. See, you hold the dictionary which I gave you as a gift. It is almost midnight, but you still read. Who can look down on you?'

71

Another guy said, 'Yes. See us while others already graduated when they are twenty-five to twenty-six years old. But we are still working a seller. But we study at night school. He will become an engineer. I will be a doctor. Most important is that we must look up on ourselves.'

Mr Chan said, 'Yes. I saw you wrote lots of notes at the desks. It impressed me. Okay. Thank you both for treating me as a friend. I remember one sentence—one word awake a sleeping man. I will take your advice. Please come in, and I will ask my mother to make pancakes for you.'

'But you always go outside to buy food during the night for us. This time, let us buy for you.'

Three guys came to the coffee shop happily.

Question: Why do you tell this story?'

Reply: Because these two guys were my best friends later. One of them became really an engineer, and the other was a doctor later. Both of them were all members of a running association which I chaired later.

Question: Did they affect your life?

Reply: Yes. Affected a lot. I was a young man and followed my brother to work in Guang An. At that moment, I knew mothering. But both of them treated me as a little brother. All of us lived in the dormitory of Guang An. We already go to the platform during the night. We talked freely and had food and drinks, looking at the stars in the sky. I keep asking questions in English. They answered me patiently. In order to help me learn by myself, he gave me a small dictionary as a gift to me.

Question: That is the one you used under the road light?

Reply: Yes. I keep it until today.

Question: Why?

Reply: Firstly, it expresses our friendship among us three. Secondly, it also indicated both my friends' fighting in study. They provided me strength. Thirdly, it reminded me that both my good friends saved my face and heart when I was down.

Chapter 24

Advice to the New Generation and Old Generation Who Built the Country

'What suggestion do you have for the new generation and the old generation who built the country?'

'I am the old generation who built the country. Since 1984, I retired from the politics area, until today, I did not feel "retirement". I have never ever stopped reading and learning and work. People's life can be summarized in five stages: founded at thirty years old, known life at forty years old, know your own life given by God at fifty years old, smooth at sixty years old, and enjoy old life at seventy years old. In Singapore, the retirement age is sixty-five. This age has three features:

Firstly, still fit.

Secondly, accumulated wisdom.

Thirdly, calm.

Of course, we respect every lift planning. But I think that a sixty-five-years-old retirement is a waste for the country, a waste of wisdom for individual. People retired, brain shrinks, in order to keep healthy of body and brain, you must let the brain work and work. It will incite cells to grow. Hence, my opinion is that working will bring people healthiness, happiness, and longer life.'

For the new generation, I think they are better than the old one. They are more smart and excellent and have broad viewpoints. They were educated well, hence has better skills and more confident.

However, I have a concern. The young generation was protected well. They are cropper, and the old generation was planter. The young generation has benefits of HDB, CPF, job opportunities, and good society environments no matter at the national level or global level. Hence, I am worrying that they will lose the spirit to create and endeavour.

To our country, they lack of the creation spirit due to good income. Due to high risk and opportunity cost, our young generation lacks of such creative spirits for globalization.

For Mainland China development, we have advantages of both Chinese and English, management skills, location, and similar blood factors compared with Hong Kong, Taiwan, and Western countries. But why do we rank lower in the recent thirty years for the results in Mainland China?

Our young generation has no interest in working overseas, like Mainland China. We are better at project feasibility study, but just in the paper, without any action. They keep appointing lawyers, accountants, etc. to investigate and assess risk for two to three years. Then finally summarized into three words—KIV, 'keep in view'.

Then the Taiwanese took the chance. Factory started, and real estate projects started. We are hesitating. This is lack of adventure and creation spirits.

I have another point to remind. We carefully operate religions, like Buddha and Jesus and Islamic party of Malaysia. We have to.

Firstly, respect others' religions.

Secondly, control yourself and do not criticize others' religions.

Thirdly, be sensitive to the contents of religions, habitats, and respect one another. Do not offend others and post jokes on others.

Each day, I feel very happy to see different religious people gathering together to work, to have lunch, and to talk life in different languages.

Chapter 25

Chinese World and Revenge with Japanese

Question: Japan invaded China, and all the Southeast Asian countries are all affected, especially the Chinese. What do you feel about Japan?

Reply: This is a big question. When I worked in the Factory 10354, I saw lots of Japanese violence.

One of our friends, a piano teacher, during her new marriage with his husband, Japanese soldiers took away his husband, and he never came back until she was ninety years old. She created a song titled 'The Person I Am Missing'. This song made all people angry.

There were thirty thousand people who died during the period occupied by Japanese soldiers. Until today, there was a milestone which indicated four suffering nations.

Looked at the word of the song:

Heart was sad and tears flow

From heart and back to heart

It is bitter left alive or sad when died

No owner, where to go

No ending missing you and no ending of bitterness of leaving

Only can see the moon change but without you

Alone, nobody to tell

Severe hating, where to flow

In 1993, the piano teacher organized a concert of good education of talents for forty years. I also wrote a paper. Each time seeing her, I always recall the Japanese violence.

Question: Do you hate the Japanese?

Reply: To be frank, no. I was not hurt personally. Instead, I was given some benefits. I was a rash boy, survived and grew under Japanese protection. I earned a piece of earning for my mother. I also learned a lot of Japanese.

Japan is a striving nation. They are a single ethics and language, high level of team spirit. A Harvard professor wrote a book titled Japan No. One, shocking the whole world, including Western and Asian leaders. It led to a style of learning Japan.

Question: Do you suggest Singapore to learn Japan?

Reply: Yes, we should learn from the USA, Japan, and Germany. In the twentieth century, Japan developed fast. Today's China is that period's Japan. After World War II, made in Japan is equal to bad goods. Then they started R&D. In the twenty-first century, China is great. The product from low end to high end, from copy to created, China can produce like Xiao Mi and the highway system.

USA still is a leader in the world. Hence, Singapore should learn from all other developed countries. However, the internal battle in Japan in the recent twenty years stopped their development. Japan has two shortcomings:

1. Japanese is introvert, sad, and elegant people. Hence, they are a loser in the international communication.

2. Japanese is a coward in the history. They cannot acknowledge their invasion in China and other Asian countries during World War II. Hence, they are going to die in their single island. What they did during the World War II made their two new generations carry the crime for more than ten years. Japanese felt imbalanced, for that today's China developed better than Japan, which made Japanese ashamed. They did not learn Germany, who reflected and faced toward World War II. Japanese did the other way instead. They felt they were great in the past and felt proud of that.

The reflection by Germany made them be respected and that the 'Made in Germany' indicates best-quality products.

Chapter 26

Expand the Respect of the Aged in One's Family to That of Other Families

Question: Chairman, according to materials, you were born on 5 November 1932 in Singapore. During your politics career, any other association you worked for?

Reply: There were many, but I cannot remember clearly. But the following two were created by me.

1. Singapore Action Group of Elders (SAGE)

2. Jogging Association of Singapore

Question: You have done lots of work. Why create SAGE? People think that the SAGE is established by the government, but not sponsored by the government. What is the motivation?

Reply: The motivation is to expand the respect of the aged in ones family to that of other families.

Question: What is the principle of the SAGE?

Reply: SAGE is not a business or religion purpose association, but a mufti-ethic and charitable association.

It mainly provides different services for elders including educations and consultancy and amusements.

After SAGE, I further established the following:

1. SAGE hotline, each day picked up phones of elder people

2. SAGE training centre in 1993, which provided training for the elder people and their families

The SAGE training centre was granted NCSS charitable position.

Questions: SAGE seems non-existent today.

Reply: Very sorry, SAGE does not exist. It can be summarized that SAGE was non-existent due to the activities which did not meet the expectations of elders.

Question: What happened to the Singapore running club?

Reply: I established the running association in 1974. I am still the chairman until today. I would like to pass it to the young men, but they loved my leader spirit. I am also the Olympic Games associate chairman.

Question: Any other association that you worked for?

Reply: Cannot remember so much but confirmed the following associations:

Judo

Swimming

Taxi drivers

Olympic games

Telephones

Running

Manjusri Middle School

Chinese hospital

TCM

BUDA

Dancing lady

Ren Ci Hospital

Question: How come you love such associations so much?

Reply: This is my nature. I will help as much as I can. Grassroots, grassroots, and grassroots that I love.

Chapter 27

Devil Hidden in Details

As Water Can Float a Boat, So Can It Swallow the Ship

Question: As an old politician who contributed to build the country, do you still care about the politics of Singapore?

Reply: Of course, I care very much.

Question: Why?

Reply: Because I believe not only me but all the old politician who contributed to build the country and cherish the current Singapore. We cannot allow anybody to ruin our country. Although in business, one saying—the rich cannot last for three generations—we must let our country, Singapore, and break such rule. We will make our nation and our people rich and powerful forever.

Question: Recently, Mr Lee Hsien Loong called for the young generation to vote wisely. They should vote based on the results/performance of politician. Do not use votes as a way to punish unsatisfactory officers. It will be dangerous.

Reply: His opinion is correct. People are the water who can make the ship flow but also can swallow the ship. I am not worried about the critical decisions by the government, neither about the execution of our bureau. I am worrying about that devil hidden in the details.

Question: Can you elaborate more?

Reply: The big advantage of the democracy is the monitoring system. One is the counterparty party monitors the ruling party. The other one is the voters monitor both counterparty and ruling parties.

To be frank, politicians must take good care of the people. Our party's execution and capability are excellent. All kinds of social international relationships were good. As an old generation of politicians, I am willing to remind the ruling party that it must pay much more attention to the details and to try to provide what the people expect rather than to lead to their complaints. Otherwise, you will lose your votes.

Question: Could you please explain more?

Reply: On 18 January 2015, ZaoBao published that the government will help the shoppers in Little India who are affected by the forbidden alcohol drinks. The background is that riots and civil commotions happened in Little India. Hence, the government issued the policy to forbid the alcohol drinks.

The Little India was ever my ruling area. I take care of this area very much. After publishing the news, my earlier voters reported to me, 'Is it because the Indian leader would like to protect Indian and take this chance to win more votes?'

Such sensitive feeling existed in many Singaporean mind. Some people will say currently, the leaders from India are more than Chinese. Will the Indian be the first leader in Singapore one day?

The first glance will consider such case as a racialism idea. Hence, the government does not want to discuss it as a topic. However, no discussion does not mean no existence. Like Malaysia, always somebody asks whether the Chinese can be appointed as the first leader of the country. The answer is no. It is due to the ratio of each races. The imbalance will cause a mess later.

Hence, for us, the proposal to help the Little Indian shoppers must be executed carefully and consider other races' feelings at the same moment.

1 April onwards, the new policy of forbidding alcohol drinks will be effective.

This new policy is unsatisfactory to all elders. My haircutter asked me to say no for them. 'Going to drink with friends is the happiest times per day. Drinking at home will make my wife angry. Drinking outside is forbidden by the government. Why are we controlled in such a tight way?'

Our officer also heard lots of unsatisfactory voices. But our officer further explained, 'Uncle, you still can drink in coffee shops. The key word is that 10:00 p.m.–7:00 a.m. are not allowed to drink.'

See, if we say 'can drink but just the timing', people will understand more. Remember, the misunderstanding will cause you to lose votes.

In fact, the investigation results showed that the elder people support more the new policy.

One saying—how to turn bad thing to a good thing? Our government should also bear this in mind. I observed that Singapore people are converting the new policy of forbidden alcohol drinks to a new drinking culture. Our people will be trained to have a good habit of drinking. 'Happily drink, control the quantity, happily go home, and not affect others.'

Question: Chairman, it is not easy. How come you still care about grassroots people so much?

Reply: Chairman Mao said, 'Come from the people and go back to the people.' This is what I did, also what the whole old generation of politicians did. The politician must pay much attention to people continuously. They should not separate from the people.

Question: Recently, during the election period, other parties challenged the People's Action Party. They targeted Tanjong Pagar. What do you think about this?

Reply: Yes. Next election must be held before the Chinese New Year of 2017. According to forecast, the election will be held on 9 June 2016. Primer Lee reminds our people this is a tough fighting and swears that People's Action Party will win in every area.

I support this great attitude. Our old generation all expected the young generation will achieve more success than us. All Western people and Taiwanese think Singapore is dictated by one party. But is that the truth? It is not.

In the past elections, we have clear statistical numbers of votes for votes of People's Action Party members. Hence, if someone says that the People's Action Party rules the Singapore dictated rather than democracy, it is not the truth.

However, I have to remind. People will change. The structure of voters will also change. The young generation was educated well and chaotic. The ruling party cannot ignore. Do not make people feel that you are proud. For example, there is a high-level minister who recently criticized the counterparty as a loser who lost for the past three times. That secretary of the counterparty frankly said, 'Yes, I acknowledged that I am a loser. You are a winner. But I will persist for myself. I am proud of that.' Once this statement appeared, the minister is going to lose his votes.

The devil really hides in the details. Be careful. Do not lose the returned 'cherishness' due to carelessness.

Initially, an excellent and capable man, Hou Yongchang, has a straightforward and decisive characteristics. He was the leaders of the officers. However, when he talked to voters, he looked impatient. As a result, he lost the authority of Potong Pasir for thirty years.

Another, Dr Xue Aimei, is extraordinary and profound. However, she washed her hands after shaking with the fish-shop owner. The story was speculated by the counterparty. As a result, she lost the voting.

Both of these candidates are capable leaders. But Singapore lost the chance of being served by them. That is a pity.

When Mr Lee Kuan Yew came back from England, he was also very far from the people. However, he is a legend person in the messy world. He created the People's Action Party. He led the Singapore politics. Although his local language is not very good, he has lots of capable supporters around him. Our old generation of the politician are close to grassroots and people. People also loved us.

We must be much careful. The devil hides in the details always.

Question: Chairman Chan, you have been in charge of one district for more than twenty years. Even after retirements, you still care about our country. I know you led people to celebrate the new water production. Today, do you have anything you want to say for your people?

Reply: Yes. I have a lot to say and also some reflection.

Firstly, I would like to bow to all my voters, leaders, and other officers in the district. I, a non-university graduate without any background, ruled the district for more than twenty years. I would like to say appreciated, appreciated, and appreciated.

All I can do is limited. Without your efforts, your loyalty, you support, and your strength, I cannot make it. That is a good history which was written by us together. That is our common memory.

Secondly, it is our party's task to improve people's life, to set up new living equipment. You know, human beings are not perfect. I have lots of shortcomings. Due to limited resources, I did not take care of the living equipment or even offended someone. Although it is the past, I apologize here.

One major work in the past is to visit my people. I always go to their homes to know their needs. I always go to food courts to talk to them. It should be done always rather than only during the election period. Moreover, you must visit your people more frequently and honestly. People have a feeling. They can feel whether it is honest or not.

Our old generation of politician loves to be a friend at the first glance. The modern politician loves media, like emails, headphones, Facebook, and blogs.

No matter old or new generations, new or old methods, the politician can never forget, 'come from the people and go back to the people', to be more careful. The devil hides in the details.

Section

"Looked at Peers"

Chapter 28

Lee Kuan Yew and His Dialect Policy

Question: May I know your opinion on the leaders whom you worked previously?

Reply: Comments? No. no. I am just 'a nobody' rather than a core VIP. I do not think it is a comment. It should be my feeling about them. Firstly, I do not want to say the great achievements of them. Secondly, I also do not think I can say better than the reporters/experts. Hence, I just talked about some stories when I worked with such great men in the past.

Question: That is great. This is what the people want. Please talk about Mr Lee Kuan Yew first.

Reply: As mentioned earlier in this book, I met Mr Lee Kuan Yew when I was young and worked in HSBC. We became friends at that moment.

He can speak English and Guangdong dialect. He cannot speak Fujian and other dialects. He knows the local high-level culture rather than grassroots.

However, he had a great dream at that moment. He was confident and always wanted to win. Such powerful characteristics and born leader feature impressed me.

As a grassroots politician, I personally summarized the following achievements of Mr Lee Kuan Yew.

Firstly, the green planting project in Singapore, which all the nation is proud of and other countries are jealous of.

I believe that all the travellers from airport to downtown will be surprised by the wide green planting on the way. Even as Singaporeans, we are proud of that. This is a screenshot of the garden city. Mr Lee Kuan Yew persistently and decisively implemented such planning. He set November as planting month. Each year, he plants trees by himself. During the period, all the trees are discounted at half. Initially, people can see the Terrance residential real estate's plans with the signature of the officer of this district. Moreover, the officer can have four hundred tax deductions.

The green planting project of Singapore is not a political show. It is a national policy. Each year, there were lots of budget. It also involved all people. The degree, wideness, and sustainability of the green planting project as well as its impact on people's life are the first creation in the world. It deserves to be listed as a 'cultural heritage'.

Secondly, the water of life drinking water project.

As known, Singapore's drinking water is provided by Malaysia all along. It is also a boring political topic. That is just Mr Lee Kuan Yew's social method to maintain Malaysia's water source all along. At the same moment, Singapore kept study and almost can produce sufficient drinking water to ourselves.

Currently, Singapore has the following water sources:

1. Johor Bahru

2. Created small or big gutter way in order to collect rains

3. Developed new water technics

4. Filtering seawater

Elder men like me all have the experience of carrying water from far away. People always quarrel due to queue order. Today, when you turn on the tap, the water flows. This is not natural. This is our leader together with lots of engineers devoted for more than ten years. I would like to remind that we need to cherish water. Water is life source.

Thirdly, multiculture and magnanimous human culture project.

Mr Lee Kuan Yew understands that multiculture, multireligions are critical for Singapore. In today's Singapore, different races of people can live peacefully together. No matter in the food courts or bus or the MRT or everywhere, the major four races lived peacefully together. It is not naturally like that. It is due to long-run management.

Fourthly, creating two language projects.

Mr Lee Kuan Yew's two language project was debated and criticized due to historical reason. But the debate is less than earlier as time goes.

This two-language policy is more for Chinese. The government policy is that English is the first mother tongue, and Chinese is the second.

Such project produced lots of people with excellent English but worse Chinese. However, compared to Hong Kong, Taiwan, and Malaysian, Singapore Chinese have better language skills. In the future, if they can improve their Chinese, they will be more competent. If considering the communication with China, Singapore Chinese will have clear competence. Hence, this is a successful project/ policy.

Mr Lee Kuan Yew' another language project is Chinese. It has been more than thirty years till now.

Initially, from more Chinese and less dialect, now no dialect, only Chinese. Such policy caused lots of debates. Until today, lots of elder men who can speak dialect also feel unhappy. They cannot understand why encouraging both English and Chinese, and they need to stop the dialect?

Question: What kinds of dialects can you speak?

Reply: I am from Nan Hai. I can fluently speak Fujian, Chaozhou, Kejia, and Hainan dialects.

Question: Due to your dialects and grassroots background, will you also refuse the English and Chinese policy?

Reply: Yes. I reserve my own opinion.

Question: Why? Can you explain more?

Reply: I am not a language expert. I have not studied. I believed that Mr Lee Kuan Yew and his language experts investigated. According to my experience of dealing with different races and learning languages, I would like to summarize as below:

1. Dialect is actually mother tongue. Learning dialect mainly completed from family or environment around.

2. Hence, learning dialect is natural and easy. My several dialects including the Malay were learned via the natural way. I remember a Japanese musician, Dr Shinichi Suzuki, found that the language-learning process of a child is listen, copy, and repeat. Dialect learning is also like that.

3. Mr Lee opined that people's energy, time, and capability are limited. It is not easy to learn both English and Chinese well. If still requiring children to learn dialects, it will drag their progress. Through my own experience and many dialect races, such idea might be lack of solid foundation. I guess Mr Lee has no experience of learning dialects. He does not know or does not believe dialect learning is easy. For voting, Mr Lee

studied Fujian dialect and Chinese. It is difficult for him. Hence, he thinks learning dialect will be difficult for ordinary people.

4. Encouraging English Chinese project harmed a lot the dialect speakers. They do not understand all along why we voted for you, but you cancelled our freedom to speak dialects. Why do this? Is it necessary?

   I just have one suggestion that it is time for us to reconsider the dialect policy.

5. As you know, every dialect has its own rich meanings and language style. The basic structure is the same as Chinese. If experts abstract the refinements, it will be absorbed into Chinese. Language is not static. It is dynamic instead. You could stop Singapore to use dialect but cannot stop the dialects in the places around like Hainan, Guangzhou, Fujian, Shan Tou, Hong Kong, and Taiwan.

Each day, how many people come into Singapore from Malaysia and speak dialects with Singaporean. How can you stop them?

Question: Then any suggestion?

Reply: Smiling, I just suggest that it is time to reconsider the policy about dialect.

Chapter 29

Dr Du JinCai

Question: Next, whom you want to discuss?

Reply: Let us talk about Dr Du JinCai.

He was a vice chairman and also minister of education bureau as well as NUS headmaster. He invited me to support his election because he knows I am good at dialect and present in grassroots language. People loves to hear. I spoke Chao Zhou dialect or sang some songs in dialect. One paragraph is as below.

'What are you doing here? I come here for emperor. Emperor has been taken by someone else. I will cook noodle.'

Dr Du likes my style of dealing with people. He has a PhD and is well educated. He is straightforward and profound. He is one of the persons whom I can argue with. He is enthusiastic. Dr Du is patient about the party, and he also takes care of party members. He seldom uses ironic word to criticize them.

Question: As spread, 'It will be a puzzle forever.' On 30 May 1959, the People's Action Party won forty-three among fifty-one seats. At night of the election, White Cloth People said that twelve members had a meeting in Mr Lee's law office and decided to vote for Mr Lee Kuan Yew or Wang YongYuan as the premier of the party. White

Cloth People said that, but finally the voting result was 6:6. Dr Du Jincai voted a special vote for Mr Lee Kuan Yew, which decided him as a leader for thirty-one years. The puzzle is whether there was a voting process.

Reply: That is due to people's curiosity or ill wishing or wishing a messy world. I do not care about the truth so much. According to White Cloth People page 171, 'Wang Bangwen insisted that there was a voting process.' At that moment, he was a paid secretary. Hence, he cannot attend the voting. But he insisted that he attended the voting process.

White Cloth People cited Mr Lee Kuan Yew's statements that 'I do not understand why Wang Bangwen and Du Jincai said so.' I do not remember such a voting process. On the same page, 拉惹勒南 confirmed that 'there was no voting process because it is not necessary to do so.' Yi Runtang also thought so. He said, 'The candidate for the leader is obvious and no doubt. If there was a voting process. It must be among Mr Lee Kuan Yew, Dr Du Jincai, and Wang Yongyuan, a central leading circle.'

Dr Du Jincai said, 'I voted for Mr Lee Kuan Yew because Wang Yongyuan is not sufficiently steady. I counted the numbers of votes in front of all people. I used my own voting authority as a chairman for Mr Lee Kuan Yew. Hence, he became the leader.'

The truth is so clear. But White Cloth People page 170 cited the email correspondence between Mr Lee Kuan Yew and Dr Du Jincai published on 19 July 1961 in a newspaper. The People's Action Party failed in the supplementary voting in An Shun. Mr Lee Kuan Yew wrote to the chairman of the party at that moment and proposed to resign from the premier. Dr Du replied that he remembered that central committee consistently voted for Mr Lee and were confident for his leading of the government and the party.

That is why White Cloth People descried that 'it will be a biggest puzzle forever in the development of People's Action Party.'

Assuming that if there is voting process, people need not be surprised. That is just the execution of democracy. Even Mr Lee Kuan Yew won the premier's position due to the one vote of Dr Du as the chairman. Nobody should interpret it too much or care too much. It will not damage the prestige of Mr Lee.

Assuming that if there is no such a voting process, Mr Lee also enjoys popular confidence and is like the sun in mid-sky all along.

Chapter 30

Wang Bangwen

Question: I heard that you are closest to Mr Wang Bangwen.

Reply: Yes. I can say without any reservation that I understand his knowledge, characteristics, capability, and behaviours. I admired him very much.

In earlier years after I joined the People's Action Party as the secretary, Wang Bangwen visited me in Guang An Company and invited me to work in the party's Neil Road headquarters. It made me feel that I am paid attention to. I was moved by his honesty and invitation.

Later, I was appointed as vice secretary of the organization. We actively selected candidates for the party.

After that, I was appointed as senator of legislation. In the party, I was a subordinate of Wang Bangwen. In the government, I am his boss.

It is strange. I am very open and love to make friends. But Mr Wang Bangwen is quiet and does not talk too much. But we became very good friends, long-term partners.

Our golden friendship started from the 1950s. Both of us have no change in our personalities in the past fifty years. He is a guest in our Saturday lunch gathering. Whenever I talked this and that with others, he always smiled and kept quiet, from the beginning to the end. I admire him.

Wang Bangwen worked in Zun Kong Middle School in Kuala Lumpur earlier. Hence, you can guess his Chinese is really good. He graduated from NUS. Hence, he is a typical person educated well by both Western and Eastern with good English and Chinese. He was loyal to our party and the leader of our party. His personality of calm, steady, and a good listener made him an excellent secretary and contributed a lot to our party and nation.

His wife, Chen CuiE, was also a central committee member of the party. She is open. She is also one of a few persons who debated with Mr Lee Kuan Yew at the meeting. Wang Bangwen was embarrassed in the middle of them.

Wang Bangwen loved his wife deeply. But unfortunately, his wife died, and he was hurt and kept quiet. Good friends always would like to introduce new girlfriend to him, but he always refused. Hence, he has not married again.

When I went to his old house, I saw all the staff of his wife kept totally original at home. Wang Bangwen's love lasts forever.

In fact, he treated his friends also like that. One of the leaders of the initial socialism party died. I saw Wang Bangwen went to the ancestral temple to mourn him.

Chapter 31

Dr Wu Qingrui

Question: I heard that Dr Wu Qingrui is really good at calculating. Nickname is Iron Abacus?

Reply: Iron Abacus refers to the following:

1. He is bean-counting.

2. He is too stingy to pull out a hair.

One time, when he competed for the voting and felt thirsty, he only paid 0.30 dollar for his own water, and all the other colleagues paid by themselves. At that moment, I was on-site. I thought this guy does not know how to behave in society. But people are positive and thought this kind of person is suitable to be the finance minister.

Dr Wu is an economist, a typical well-educated person. He was a senior officer before he joined our party. His election area is Chinatown. Dr Wu cannot speak Cantonese. Even the simple regards in Chinese during voting process, he also needs to make notes in English for the pronunciation in Chinese. His Chinese is in a strange tone.

Because I know dialect and from grassroots, I was invited by him to his Chinatown areas to show my Cantonese and dialects skills. I was also appointed to be a member of the management in finance department. Hence, I closely worked with Dr Wu.

He is very smart in big-issue but naive in non-critical things. He treated our members friendly. He invited me to his modern house for many times to listen to his speech about macroeconomics. We all respect him as a lecturer, a professor. Of course, he deserved to hold a PhD in economics.

Section

'Looked at Relatives and Friends'

Chapter 32

Nephew

Hu Yao Wei

The original content was written in English. Please refer to page 168 in the book for this chapter.

Chapter 33

Best Friend

Dr Lui Hah Wah Elena

The senior lady who is the generation of establishing Singapore. Her poem is 'Wood and Summer 2015'

Thanks, Mr and Mrs Chan, the couple invited me to write this poem. It simply expresses my feeling and thoughts rather than a literary poem.

Firstly, it commemorates our two families' friendship for five generations. I also appreciate their rich life experience, which brought us joy.

Secondly, it is about our old life experience and appreciation.

This piece of article omitted the detailed contents. Thanks for your understanding and wish you be safe, healthy, and joyful.

The Luck of Singapore Nations is always good,
the friendship in XI MU Street continues generation by generation;

The plants in the Mountain of Pearl will be green each seasons,
the service of welfare department will make each family safe;

The senior persons in Mao De Street smiles and smiles,
the people celebrates the victory of drinking
waters at MacRitchie Reservoir;

Lion Dancing in Xi Hu Street appears each year,

Dragon and phoenix brings spring each seasons;

The establishing nation generation loves to use the set,

medical set provides the debates;

The young girl sleep early and get up early,

the water used three times is re-filtered to the market;

Milk tea vegetables, rice and fresh fruits,

to have a simple meal with less meat;

Walk and dance in the morning and bird sings,

meet and chat with good friends happily;

MRT and Bus can reach everywhere,

make the best of everything and protect the environment;

Hot whether always changes suddenly,

cold and hot interchanges and leads to flu easily.

To know how to protect and learn the unknown things,

adjust properly and keep simply dressed;

Science developed so fast and changed the world each day,

the computer is advanced and we need to seize time to learn;

The hour consultant guides social workers,

work hard continuously and both learner

and teacher improve together;

The doctor knows the world via the internet,

astronomy, Mathematics and physics, art is long but life is short;

A Brief Introduction of Dr Lui Hah Wah Elena

1968, graduated from Hong Kong Chinese University, majored in social work

1974, immigrated to Singapore

1983, became a Singapore citizen

1975–2012, worked in NUS Education School

1977, activated the 'senior' to highlight healthy and graceful life after retirements, voted to retire but not rest

Chapter 34

Best Friend

Captain Peter Ho Kia Tuang

Please refer to page 172 for the original version in English.

Chapter 35

A Friend in Need Is a Friend Indeed

Question: Could you please introduce the photo that shows you and your twelve friends?

Reply: Yes, it was taken in December 2014. I was injured in my right leg during the Nation Day in 2014. I was hospitalized in the ICU for several days. Then I went back home in a wheelchair. During that period, relatives and friends including the colleagues when I worked in the party and from our international school sent regards to me. It was painful in the leg but sweet in my heart.

In December 2014, a bunch of friends came to my home and visited me. I was so happy. We gathered and chatted happily for two hours. I totally forgot my leg issue. We used smartphone to take the photo of this moment for everyone's smile.

In the photo (please refer to page 175 in the original book), the second row from left to right are Lee Chongguan, Wu Miaoxiong, Lee Jinshan, Xie Lizhen, Zhu Tuanhao, Lee Chongnan, Sun Meihua, and Xiao Haoyi.

The first row from left to right are Lin Ken, He Peizhu, Chen Zhenai, Mr. Chan, Zhong Wenling, and Xu Ludi.

He Peizhu is an ex-city senator. She wrote a poem for this event.

Mr Chan, My Old Friend
by He Peizhu

Aims to help people for society, achieves contribution to education;
Planting in the rural area is difficult, do not say pioneer is a fool;
If there no prior people's hard work, how
we have today's fruitful results;

It is an honor to have a bachelor degree, persistent
hard working can create a heaven;
It is glory to serve to people, there is no
light if greedy of power or money;

Loyal and good word for justice, goodwill and help make you happy;

Another old friend, Zhong Wenling, is a VIP in literature. His name is Tian Liu, a famous writer of novels, poems, and dramas as well as comic dialogue. He also wrote a poem as below.

To Mr Chan, My Best Friend
by Zhong WenLing

Young and strong like a dragon, friendly
to all friends with great warm;

Working in politics with justice, solve issues and know everything;

No greedy to have money as a governor, always
keep goodwill and clear bad things;

cast aside corruption with no hesitation, be

loyal to his friends like a sun;

so messy tiny work, deal with people's issue objectively and fairly;

voting people countered difficulty, carefully solved that;

people suffering need help, try to keep peaceful heart;

suddenly hear raining at night, worrying about people's life;

Mr Chan is a firm person with justice. Almost all his old friends treated people frankly. If he found anybody cheated, he will not keep the friendship with him/her.

All his friends know that Mr Chan loves to help people. For example, he always tried to help people no matter as a governor or an individual. He helped his colleagues in the party, his relatives, and friends. He always treated his friends warmly and frankly.

by Zhong WenLing

Ms Zhong even use a more direct word and wrote the following poem:

During that unstable years,

During that year,

Young, strong and firm will,

At that moment,

116

Everyone is old friend on the same way;

Today,

Everyone is the generation who established the nation;

Ear changes, everything changing;

We are in the big storm but still stand firmly.

by Xu Ludi

High-level viewpoint;
For nations and peoples, there is a will, there is a way
by Lee Lingjing

Total Loyalty for Nation;
Strong Will for People;

by Feng Yaqing

(Please refer to the photo in page 179, Mr Chan with his good friends, including the reporter.)

(Please refer to the photo 1 in page 180, Mr Chan with his good friends chatting happily.)

(Please refer to the photo 2 in page 180, Mr Chan with his good friends gathering happily.)

(Please refer to the photo 3 in page 181, Mr Chan with his good friends. The first in the left is Wang Bangwen.)

(Please refer to the photo 4 in page 181, Mr Chan with his good friends. The middle person is Lin Qingxiang.)

(Please refer to the photo 5 in page 182, Mr Old Colleague visited Mr Chan.)

(Please refer to the photo 6 in page 182, Mr Chan with his sister and his sister's husband.)

Chapter 36

Closely Connected with Mr Chan

by Zeng Guiming

I met one great mentor in 1960. He is Yang Jianmin, an agent of Yamaha car in Singapore and Malaysia. His shop is in Mr Chan's voting district. Mr Yang invited me to work for his advertisements. One day, an old friend looked for me in the company and invited me to attend the 'volunteer singing of Che Baozhu' and published in the newspaper. The event was very successful.

In 1970, Mr Yang achieved the CEO's attention of Yamaha and was appointed as the number 1 agent of Yamaha in Singapore and Malaysia. I was appointed as a manager in Yamaha Music School.

His career developed so fast. The student numbers increased to more than 1,000 in two years only. But it also brought me trouble. The old HDB is not sufficient for the fire protection criteria. I considered and reconsidered, then dialled the number to Mr Chan as the officer of the government at that moment.

Me: Hi, Mr Chan, this is Zeng Guiming of Yamaha Music School.

Mr Chan: Yes, I know. I received your posted writings, which is about our country's music education and activities. Thank you. It was wonderful. Anything I can help?

Me: May I know which day you meet voters? I need to talk to you.

Mr Chan: Hey, bro, you can call me Chee Seng. Anything I can help? You just tell me. No need to wait until I meet voters.

Me: The old school does not meet the fire protection criteria.

Mr Chan: I will send some fireman to your school to check. They will report anything you can do to make up that.

Me: Thank you so much. You are so efficient. Admire you.

Mr Chan: No need to talk to me in that way. You contributed to education. The government should thank you. If you have difficulty, we should help. This is our responsibility. Also, you are in my voting district.

Since then, I became friends with Mr Chan, until now. It is already half a century.

During a party in 2000, I told Mr Chan this piece of memory. I thought he would say, 'Yes. Interesting.' But who knows, he said, 'Did I really do that?'

Mr Chan, you are so great!

Section

'Contribution in Education'

Chapter 37

Education for Booming Nation Creates Fortune for Next Generations

One: Mr Chan's Spirit and Territory for Education

Mr Chan was only educated in a private school for accident Chinese for several years and Yang Zheng Primary School for two to three years and middle school for 1.5 years.

It may be right that the times produce their heroes. In 1950s, the Singapore politics stage called for governors from grassroots level, such as Chen Cui'e, Peter Liu, He Peizhu, and Cao Yiying, who did not obtain a colleague education even. But all of them were loved by voters. Mr Chan is also an extraordinary example.

However, after retirement in 1984, for Mr Chan, it turned out that heroes produce their times. He changed his career path to education industry. He achieved a lot. He became the first pioneer of Singapore International Education. Then there were many followers. So as of now, there are more than thirty international schools in Singapore, so blooming!

Let us see Mr Chan's education territory:

1. 1981, established International School of Singapore (ISS)

2. 1994, established Beijing International School (BISS)

3. 1997, established Center for American Education (CAE)

Mr Chan's education background is significantly different from his education career achievements.

Moreover, there was lack of financial support.

His whole career in politics is totally not related to his education career.

So how can he obtain such great achievements in his education career?

Two: President and Employee, Cleaning and Knocking the Bell

Question: People are all curious why you selected the education industry after retiring from politics.

Reply: I sought for Dr Wu Qingrui's suggestions before I visited London. He frankly shared, 'Please just consider to establish a school which can realize your dream and wishes.'

The investigation in London widened my viewpoints. Once I came back to Singapore, no alternative idea, just would like to establish a school.

Question: However, firstly, you don't have even a college education background. Second, you have no experience of operating a school. Third, you are a businessman with lots of money. How did you find financial support?

Reply: If looking back now, I also felt I was rash. Everything happened just being pushed by a kind of impulse of motion which was brewing in my body for a long time.

It is just because I lost my education opportunity when I was a child. Such painful regret cannot be understood by others, and I suffered a lot due to having no education background. For example, 'You were educated so little. What can you do?' 'You want to borrow money from me? You have so little educational background. How can you find a job to earn money to repay me?'

Even when I was appointed to be a governor in the politics career path, I felt weaker for the education part. My political career cannot make up for my regret about the little education background. All these led to my impulse to establish an education career.

Since I was a child, I worked to raise myself. All my life path is just following my mother's advice. 'My child, please make friends extensively. You must be brave. Your friends will be our guiders and teachers.'

I indeed had no experience of establishing a school. In fact, I have no related experience for all the work I did in my life. I agree with the famous writer Lu Xun that a road is created by people's walking. Hence, relying on my faith and life experience, I never had any hesitation. After coming back from London, I started to devote to an education career.

Question: Did you discuss with your wife or with any experts? Did you have sufficient money?

Reply: No. No. I just had some savings. But I started. I visited one of my friend, a Western person who is a manager in Rothman Cigarette factory. The guy owns a vacant building near Bukit Timah. (Please refer to the picture in page 189 of the original book).

I said to him, 'Hey, bro, I would like to run a school. Can you rent your building at a cheap rate to me?' He said, 'Of course. Anyway, it was vacant for quite a long time.'

I asked further, 'How much for the rental fee?'

He said, 'You can just use. Until you earn your tuition fees, then you can pay me as you like.'

I guess he might think in his heart, Mr. Chan is just a rash man. Hopefully he can survive in the education industry.

Question: Who did you hire as a chairman? How many administrators at the beginning?

Reply: At the beginning, I just occupied one of the three rooms in the building. There was no chairman, no administrators. I myself was a true chairman and employee, in charge of cleaning and knocking the bell.

I invited two male friends who lived near to the school. They were willing to help me for free as a part-time teacher.

At the beginning, I designed the advertisements by myself. Later, I met a colleague in the Japanese factory. He helped me to design the posts. He helped to post around the school and downtown streets.

Our tuition fee is much lower than the other schools. We also did not have any admission examinations. It was quite like a basic school in a rural area.

In the infant stage, the children registered are all the ones who were deprived of education and lived around my school. I also often walk around the downtown to find the children who had nothing to do and roamed the streets or even begged. Such picture made me recall my youth. I tried to persuade their parents to allow the children to learn in my school no matter more or less tuition fee.

At the beginning, there were not enough chairs and desks. Some students sat on the ground. Even in such a bad environment, there was no child who quit. Instead, some parents of the students supported us for education and donated some money for us. We attracted more than fifty students plus their parents. The building looked too small.

Hence, I started to find a new place.

We adopted Kong Zi's 'provide education for all people without discrimination'. Kong Zi is one of greatest Chinese ancient educators.

Very soon, more than 300 students registered in my school.

Question: What is the name of your first school?

Reply (laughing): Right. It was called the First School. I was a senator and held other titles in politics. Such background provided me helps and convenience. I looked for assistance from the education bureau. The officers are all very cooperative. They found a primary school. Due to too few students, the owner cannot run it any longer. Hence, they would like to rent it out. Although the rooms are not so large, I quickly decided to rent it and also kept that ex-chairman as a teacher.

'It is necessary to have effective tools to do good work.' Once I had this rectangle school, I just felt like a bird flying.

I organized a secretary team who was in charge of all kinds of administration work. I hired a Western chairman and ten teachers. The teachers had no fixed salary, totally depending on the revenue by the end of each month. The thing that made me admire them was that all these teachers did not mind.

That was in 1986. During that period, I could not sleep well each night, always worrying about what I should do if I cannot pay the salaries to the teachers.

We adopted Kong Zi's 'provide education for all people without discrimination'. Kong Zi is one of greatest Chinese ancient educators.

Very soon, more than 300 students registered in my school. However, during the peak season, the school sources were not sufficient again. I restarted to find a third place.

Three: Lots of Trees, Birds Flying, and Flowers Blooming, Squirrels Played around the Trees

Question: Where is your third school?

Reply: To be honest, I really thank the officers in the education bureau. They provided me lots of support and assistance. I visited them again. They quickly said, 'Mr Chan, you are welcome. We appreciated your contribution to educations. You came at the right timing. We have a school near to Preston Hill. Please take a look first. If you are interested, we will cooperate with your application.

Question: That is your current headquarter?

Reply: Yes. I quickly go to Preston Hill after coming out from the education bureau. I was shocked. The school was amazing. There are two entrances. One is from Depot Road via 200 steps. The other one is from Preston Road through a walk lane. On the way, you could see lots of plants, different kinds of birds flying, and a big squirrel quickly climbed into a tree when he saw me. Such environment made me felt clean in the heart.

This is a place for ladies' education during the British ruling period. After they went back, this school changed to a local school. However, due to the location on the top of a mountain and inconvenient transportation, children and their parents were not willing to learn here. When I visited the place, I met the last class for a primary level 1 students.

But I cherished the place very much. I was not puzzled by the feng shui. However, when I looked around, I saw lots of trees, birds flying, and small lovely squirrels. I said to myself, 'Wow, this is a really good place with wonderful feng shui.'

In a very short time, I signed a contract for thirty years of this place.

I renamed it as ISS.

I knew a painter named Lin Youquan. I asked his father, a famous painter, to write the school name for me.

I appreciated Master Lin's writings and help.

We hired a capable chairwoman at that moment. We defined our school as an international school. Our students were targeted to be children of foreigners.

The chairwoman was a great woman who was really an expert from England education. Later, his husband was appointed to work in India. She had to resign and followed his husband to live in India for several years.

After that, these couple went back to Singapore. She was one senior member of management committee of ISS all along. Later, she was hired by an international school charting bureau. She investigated for educations all over the world. Once her tenure was done, I quickly hired her back to my ISS.

The decoration work of Preston Hill started quickly. Students, their parents, old friends, including the team members of old generation from establishing the nation came and helped. Even some old friends reminded me that 'due to 200 steps and inconvenient transportation here, it is very difficult to find students.'

However, there is a saying that one man's meat is another man's poison. Hence, I believe different people love different things.

For a local person, parents think that climbing 200 steps is dangerous for their children and troublesome. However, for Western parents, they think that climbing 200 steps is really good to their children's health. Moreover, they love the adventure feeling.

Another more important reason is that there was no private international school at that moment in Singapore.

ISS was very popular.

Four: ISS Suited ISS

Question: Can I say that your education career is on the right track since then? Everything is smooth after that?

Reply: Yes, it is a huge breaking point. We rebuild the lane to a wide road, which makes it easy to drive a car in. We had an international education expert as our chairwoman. Achieving all these is not so smooth.

Question: Please provide some examples.

Reply: We suddenly received a letter from International Syllabus Service in a short-term ISS as well. They said they would sue us for violating their name. Their tone in the letter was really firm. Shortly, their CEO visited Singapore and made an appointment with me to meet at the airport.

The CEO directly said, 'Mr Chan, do you know you used ISS, which was our short-form name used for several decades. Your behaviour seriously violated us. If you do not refrain from using ISS, you must take the responsibility by yourself.'

I heard and was scared. To be honest, I had never ever known there was another institution named ISS in the world. Moreover, this institution happily provided all kinds of international education materials for international schools all over the world, also in charge of recruitments of teachers and monitoring of the schools. More than that, it was also the only one authority institution in the education area.

133

On one hand, I expressed carefulness. On the other hand, I firmly replied, 'Mr CEO, sorry for any incontinence caused. However, please let me explain the truth. Our school's full name is International School of Singapore. Its short form is ISS or ISS International School. Singapore is a society with strong legislation system. This name has been approved and registered in the Singapore Education Bureau. Our name and your organization name are not same to each other. And the meaning of each character in the full name between us is also totally different. How can you say we violated yours?'

That CEO was angry. But he calmed down and said, 'Mr Chan, what I referred to is ISS, these three letters. You seem to mislead me. Let me summarize. I inform you right now verbally that please cancel your school name of ISS now. Otherwise, my organization will freeze you from the recruitments of the teachers and education materials.'

Question: Did he really freeze you?

Reply: Yes. That ISS froze my ISS for several years. But they never ever sued us. Maybe they do not want to screw up the relationship with the Singapore government due to this stuff. They know my background with the Singapore government. After another several years, they saw our achievements, then they agreed us to use ISS.

Question: It seems that there is one lucky star who always takes care of you.

Reply: It is not one lucky star. Instead, it is a lucky heart. My mother told me the advice when I was just five or six years old, 'My child, you must be brave and make lots of friends. Friends will be your guiders and supporters.'

This advice helped me everywhere and every time. I did it.

I am not a guy believing in God, but I really feel like there is a big hand behind me to support me whenever I bravely fight. I remember that one day, I took a bus. It is too crowded. I stood on one step at the bus gate and only could use one hand to hold the pole. If I fell, I would break my head. But I recalled my mother's advice and held the pole tightly. However, a moment I was almost falling, there was a big hand behind me that pushed me to stand again. I was pushed into the bus. There were too many people in the bus. I really could not tell who helped me.

In my life, there is always a big hand behind me to support me whenever I almost fell. But that hand only helps brave people.

Chapter 38

What Is the International School?

This year was 2014. IT was expanding so fast. It was really that people no longer need to step out of their house and know everything all over the world. No matter in history or current time, no matter you are here or there, you can communicate in voice or by written media in one minute.

However, it is ironic, I asked what the international school is. Many people cannot answer. Or some answer is not for the question. Even the people in education industry cannot reply a good concept.

Someone said, 'It is a school related to international affairs.'

Someone said, 'It is based on English?'

Someone said, 'It is a school that provided joined modules with other country's schools.'

Someone said, 'It is a school that provided IB courses.'

In fact, international school covers lots of meanings. In the following parts, we will introduce ISS and BISS. Then you can understand a clear concept.

Chapter 39

ISS International School, Singapore

ISS has two campuses.

One is located around Preston Campus, on Preston Road.

Kindergarten, primary school, and middle school are located in the Paterson campus.

Overall, the number of students keeps consistently around 700 to 800. There are around 250 among of them who are in high school, 160 in middle school, and 330 in primary and kindergarten.

Due to the scope of the two campus, we cannot accommodate more students. Right now, ISS group is developing new campus building which will be competed in two years. Then we will accommodate 1,500 to 1,700 students.

All the teachers in ISS came from all over the world who must be trained by IB courses.

Currently, there are around fifty high school teachers, twenty middle school teachers, and fifty-five primary and kindergarten school teachers.

Accounting, administration, maintenance, HR, marketing, and IT together have around fifty staffs.

Hence, the operating cost of ISS is much higher than expected.

Chapter 40

ISS International School Yearbook 2013–2014

For Mr Chan's message to ISS International School yearbook 2013–2014, please refer to page 204 for the original version in English.

Chapter 41

Message from the Head of School for Yearbook 2013–2014

Please refer to page 206 for the original version in English.

Chapter 42

ISS International School 2014–2015

Please refer to page 207 for the original version in English.

Chapter 43

Message from the High School Principal

Please refer to page 209/(153) for original version in English.

Chapter 44

Message from the Middle School Principal

Please refer to page 210/(91) for the original version in English.

Chapter 45

Message from the Elementary School Principal

Please refer to page 212/(7) for the original version in English.

Chapter 46

Beijing BISS International School 2014

Please refer to page 216 for the photo.

Chapter 47

One Night in Beijing

Question: According to the materials, you created BISS in 1994. Could you please explain why you established school overseas? Why China? Why Beijing?

Reply: there is a popular song, 'One night in Beijing, I left lots of love.' Although that is just a popular song, it reflects the Beijing as a country's capital attracts people's attention so much.

My trip in Beijing also left lots of love. I had the feeling of going back home finally.

Firstly, I am a person who does not like to stop. When my career in the education industry reaches a stage, I would like to create something more. Singapore is a small country. If I only focused on Singapore, the room for development is limited, career like floating in the opposite direction with the water flowing. If not improving, it will be worse. Hence, I will change. Change will bring improvement.

Secondly, we are all Chinese. Our grand-grand generations came to Nanyang and settled down in Singapore, then became Singaporeans. However, our first home town can be said as China. We, like the salmon, will swim back to the birthplace to raise the next generation.

Thirdly, Beijing is the capital of China. It is a centre of China's economy, politics, and culture. All over the world pays attention to Beijing. I was thinking that if I can occupy the market in Beijing, then it is easier for me to occupy big and small cities later.

Question: Did you have any relationship networks in Beijing? For example, relationship with governors?

Reply: No. I had no friends in Beijing from rich people or governors. Nothing I knew about Beijing at that moment. I just brought two trust friends, Chen Zhiyin and Lin Naiyan. We negotiated with the Beijing Chaoyang District education department for three times. Then we signed the contract for the school located in An Zhen Xi Li.

Question: It is totally incredible. Like this case, it is supposed to be lasting for two to three years and signed by more than ten governors. How did you do?

Reply: Even today, such application is also very complicated. We, three persons, contacted our own networking respectively. I was associated Olympic chairman of Singapore, hence, contacted the relevant bureau in Beijing. Lin Naiyan contacted the Beijing education department. Chen Zhiyin contacted the Xin Huashe. Finally, we found the school.

Lin Naiyan is an educator. We hired him as our education consultant. Chen Zhiyin is an outstanding reporter who reported on sixteen Olympic Games. Hence, we hired him as our marketing consultant.

During the first conversion with the old chairman of the school, he shared with us the basic requirements. During the second round, he arranged the governors in Chaoyang District. In the third round, we met the education high-level officers. The contents are very interesting. It can be summarized as below.

Education department: What is the international school?

Reply: It is a modern education system. From kindergarten to high school, all the materials and textbooks are provided by the international education service centre. All the teachers will be foreigners. They must be trained by IB. All the major courses will be taught in English. But we will teach Chinese, French, Japanese, depending on the students' nationality.

Education Department: What kind of content in the textbook? Any religions? Any Western values?

Reply: To be honest, I am worrying about these more than you. Based on Singapore international education experiences, we did not find any listed contents. ISS students came from all over the world. It is sort of a small national union.

Our school in Beijing will also copy the model of ISS in Singapore. In summary, all the materials do not contain something of a culture violation or cleaning brains.

The style is different from the traditional education system. We encourage more creativity and independent thinking as well as more communications between students and teachers. We warmly invited you and your colleagues to Singapore to investigate our ISS in Singapore.

Question: They really were persuaded by you and approved your applications?

Reply: I am not good at speaking. I just talk frankly. I think they trusted me. However, this is a big case for the education department. They cannot approve so fast and so easily. Let us forecast the results.

Firstly, we thank our nation, Singapore. Singapore has good reputation in the world. Since 1978, Mr Deng Xiao Ping visited Singapore. He also suggested China learn from Singapore. Hence, I think they trust Singapore. As a Singapore ex-governor, they trust me as well.

Secondly, ISS provided a good example for them.

Thirdly, the Beijing education department is really intelligent. There was no international school in China at that moment, but I know they did lots of research and knew well about the international school. Hence, we shake hands during the dinner. We became good friends as well.

One night in Beijing, it was far more than leaving lots of love. It should be said, I found my home town.

Chapter 48

As Long as One Has a True Friend, He Is Close Even When Far Away

Question: When I was in Beijing in October 2014. I met two of your old friends, Gao YuChen and Li Ming. They said that this book is in the process. They volunteered to write a chapter for you. Very fast, just in two weeks, they emailled me the drafts. May I know your impression about these two friends?

Reply: They are not only old friends to me, they are also builders of our ISS. Hence, I deeply thank them.

Gao Yuchen was appointed as a high-level officer in the Chaoyang education district. He is a very senior educator. After his retirement in 2011, I hired him as our group consultant.

Li Ming was appointed as the associated dean in the Beijing City committee research office. After retirement in 2007, I also hired him as our group consultant.

Our relationship in twenty years not only built our education for booming nations and next generations but also built our solid friendship. Just like the poem says, 'As long as one has a true friend, he is close even when far away.'

Question: Do you have any difficulty to communicate with both at the first meeting?

Reply: Everyone prepared well about the difficulties. First, China's opening policy speeded up during 1992. We entered into Beijing in 1993–1994. It seems still too early.

Second, the international school concept is not easy to be understood by Chinese officers.

However, it is totally beyond our expectation. We can communicate very smoothly and reached an agreement. We started the decoration.

Question: During that period, any project needs to take three to five or eight to ten years to be approved. Can you share why you can make it so fast?

Reply: When we first met, I brought our educator Lin Naiyan and senior reporter Chen Zhiyin. They had Gao Yuchen and Li Ming. I did not prepare any feasibility study report. I did not consider it as a commercial project. I just would like to contribute to my home town.

Question: Sorry, excuse me. Do you think China is your home town?

Reply: Yes. Yes. In 1954, when primer Zhou En Lai attended the Asia-Africa meeting, he said that all the Chinese overseas are like the married daughters and sons of China. He welcomes them come back home at any moment. We are just the guests or the married sons of China.

When I shake hands with Gao Yuchen and Li Ming, I introduced myself in Guangdong dialect. At that moment, both of us felt so close to each other. In my mind, the following song appeared, 'Far, far in the eastern area, there is a dragon named Chang Jiang. Far, far in the eastern area, there is a river named Huang He. Black eyes, black hair, yellow skin are dragon sons forever.'

I was very excited. I said, 'I am not a businessman. I came back to make my own contribution to country. I only have insufficient money and want to establish a school. I think the education can lead to rich people, then further lead to rich country. I would like to make my own tiny contribution.'

That is it. We broke the barriers. We understood each other quite well without any communication issues.

Chapter 49

Records of Some Memories of Mr Chan in the Education Career

by Li Ming

I knew Mr Chan for more than twenty years already. He is a very firm and solid man. He is so impressive to me and gave me lots of good fluency.

In the autumn of 1993, the education department chairman invited me to meet a guest from Singapore. Chaoyang District is the largest education area in Beijing. There are more than 320 primary and middle schools.

During that night, a man of sixty-plus years old showed on time. He looked very energetic although with white hair. He saw us and quickly stepped ahead to shake our hands. After his warm regards like old friends, we had no feeling of being strangers. We quickly discussed the topic.

Mr Chan is a successful educator in Singapore. During the 1980s, Singapore economy developed fast, and lots of foreigners' children had the difficulties of education in Singapore. Mr Chan identified the timing and established the international school in Singapore on time.

Mr Chan pointed the same timing in Beijing. I am expressed by his viewpoint. Hence, we agreed to set aside one middle school to cooperate with Mr Chan.

After confirmation, Mr Chan came to Beijing for several times. We became familiar to each other. Beijing has a large area, and Chaoyang District is also complicated to a foreigner. Once, I gave him a map. He cherished the map very much.

From decoration to plating, Mr Chan always deals with by himself carefully. After one year of preparation, a school like a garden started in 1994.

Such school not only filled in the gap of Beijing education but also contributed to the Beijing's opening reform.

Later, I found that map which was decorated gracefully and hanging in the wall. In the map, there are lots of marks. It not only shows his footmarks but also shows his efforts.

In the twenty-plus years, BISS achieved proud results with the leading of Mr Chan. The admission rate kept high consistently. Many, many students graduated from BISS and enrolled in the world's famous universities.

At the same time, BISS is also open to the ordinary school which widens students' viewpoints. BISS helped training English teachers. BISS also organized lots of events with local schools, which contributed to the merging of Western and Eastern educations. BISS gained good reputations in the Chaoyang District education industry.

Mr Chan also paid much attention to the details, including the facilities of the school and communications with students and their parents. People liked him very much, and took photos with him always.

During the period, Mr Chan made lots of friends in China from local people to governor. Each time he came to Beijing, he would take the chance to talk to old friends to pick up some advice on education.

Mr Chan is modest, frank, and admirable. When he knew that the poems in stone of Beijing Yun Ju Si would be stored in Tibet, Mr Chan donated a lot of money for Yun Ju Si. His charitable heart gained him lots of respect by the people.

During China's sixtieth-year birthday in 2009, Mr and Mrs Chan were invited to Beijing for the celebration dinner and ceremony.

Today, ISS is trying to create a new chapter. BISS has provided room for joint education. In 2013, I was invited to Singapore. Mr Chan gathered us at his home. Just as I entered into his lobby, I saw a painting by Zhang Daqian. It is a pine tree. Standing in front of the painting, I had many ideas in mind. In my heart, Mr Chan is like a pine tree who will never grow old, instead always keeping firm, straight, and never fearing of snow or sun. He will be always energetic and will fight forever.

About Li Ming

1977, a student majoring in economics in Capital Economics and Trade University

1982, associate dean in the Beijing City committee research office

1990, associate district director of Chaoyang

1999, dean of Chaoyang District political office

2007, retired

Chapter 50

Message from the Chairman, BISS International School

Please refer to page 231 for the original version in English.

Chapter 51

Connecting with the Head of School

Please refer to page 233 for the original version in English.

The first photo in page 233: 2007 ISS staff visited China Education Department officers. Second from the left is the wife of the chairman of the China Education Department.

The second photo in page 233: Mr Chan with the chairman of the China Education Department.

The first photo in page 234: 2007 president Na Dan visited ISS. The lady is Mrs Chan.

The second photo in page 234: Mr Chan happily chatting with old friends.

All photos in page 235–236: BISS graduation ceremony.

Section of Attachments

Chapter 52

ISS International School

First International School Established by a Singaporean

The reports published in Chinese in the page (94–98) are all sorts of advertisements and brief introduction. All the contents were covered by the translation in above chapters.

The reports published in Chinese in the page (11–13) are a brief introduction about M. Chan, who focused on the education industry after retirement. All the contents were covered by the translation in above chapters.

Chapter 53

The Last Salute

23 March 2015

by Mr Chan

For this whole month, no matter when the handphone rings, my heart beats faster.

'How is Mr Lee Kuan Yew who is lying in the SGH ward?'

I ask, everyone asks.

I am so worrying, and everyone is so worrying.

I pray, and everyone is praying.

He is a born leader. He is the creator of modern Singapore. He is a great, brave, and intelligent soldier.

He is my supervisor of politics. We had beef noodles along the Singapore River together. We went to Malacca and Kuala Lumpur together. We had 'robbed' back the desks and chairs occupied by the socialism party together.

We fought and won our counterparty on the nation's Union Street.

He is a great man whom all of our people love and respect.

He is also an intelligent person who gained respect from all over the world.

Times pushed people to grow old. Times take away people.

However, he will be forever in all our people's heart.

Chapter 54

The Ex-President of the US Comforting Mr Chan

During the period of Mr Lee Kuan Yew's funeral ceremony, the US ex-president, Mr. Bill Clinton, patted Mr Chan.

Lightning Source UK Ltd.
Milton Keynes UK
UKHW012021040821
388278UK00001B/24

9 781543 766561